Art and Forbidden Fruit

Hidden Passion in the Life of William Morris

John Y. Le Bourgeois

L

The Lutterworth Press

The Lutterworth Press
P.O. Box 60
Cambridge
CB1 2NT

www.lutterworth.com
publishing@lutterworth.com

First Published in 2006

ISBN (10): 0 7188 3061 X
ISBN (13): 978 0 7188 3061 8

British Library Cataloguing in Publication Data
A catalogue record is available from the British Library

Printed in the United Kingdom by
Athenaeum Press, Gateshead

Contents

For Mimi

I am something of an Englishman and the words won't flow, it's one of the curses entailed on our blood and climate.

William Morris

Man is least himself when he talks in his own person. Give him a mask, and he will tell you the truth.

Oscar Wilde

Preface

William Morris, when he was twenty-two years old, fell in love with Arthur Hughes's painting, *April Love*. The picture shows a young woman turning away from her lover. For Morris, it captured perfectly the feeling of love denied that had overwhelmed him after his favorite sister married. It was the same emotion that made him a poet.

Morris bought the painting in 1856. A year later he met Jane Burden. For a year and a half he struggled with two competing visions of love before choosing the only one permissible. In April 1859 he married Miss Burden; the couple then lived for several years in a beautiful house designed by their friend Philip Webb. It was a very happy time for both of them.

Only after Morris suffered a serious illness did he question the validity of his marriage. He began writing poetry again, which he had virtually abandoned when he wed. For Morris's poetry, indeed all of his artistic expression, remained grounded in his passion for his sister, a passion that began in infancy.

Art and Forbidden Fruit explains how Morris's love for his sister evolved, how it destroyed his marriage and how it produced the great achievements of his life. For his sister was a guide to heroic behavior as well as a source of erotic emotion.

Acknowledgments

There are many individuals who have helped me write this book. Peter Cominos acted as my advisor and mentor; he approved, even though he was surprised to learn, what I was writing about. J.C. Maxwell encouraged me as I delved into the manuscripts in the Bodleian Library. Without the support of these two eminent scholars this book would not exist.

Other advisors, colleagues and friends who aided me in one way or another were: Adrian Brink, Hallman Bryant, John Corenswet, Ann Ebrecht, Edward T. Hall, Alvin Hero, Barry Hannah, Charles Israel, Francis James, Norman Kelvin, Bill Koon, Morton Kligerman, Terry Meyers, Douglas Mitchell, Marshall Patner, Philip Rief, Edward Rosenheim, Sarah Searight, Alan Schaffer, David Slater, Gardner Taplin, Thomas Verich and Seth Wolitz.

The directors and staff of the Bodleian Library, the British Library and the Victoria and Albert Museum were essential to my research; these were the three institutions where I spent most of my time and made my most important discoveries. I received considerable help also from the faculty and librarians of the several universities with which I have had the good fortune to be associated: Yale University, Tulane University, Clemson University, the University of Chicago and Temple University. In the past year, as I have brought this work to a conclusion, the staff of the library of Swarthmore College and the Swarthmore Public Library have also come to my aid.

One

He felt the separation keenly

William Morris was born to make his mark on the world. He had all the natural endowments. He was strong, energetic and emotionally alive. He was equipped with the keenest senses and a remarkable imagination. All of these qualities were evident from the very beginning.

Morris said that he could never remember a time when he did not read. At age four he was reading books written for adults, and by seven he had read all the Waverly novels, many books by Marryat and others as well. If true, this was an incredible feat. The Waverly novels of Walter Scott number twenty-nine books and three tales, and Captain Marryat wrote ten adventure stories. Whether Morris read all, or merely some, of these novels, he was a rare, literate child.

His visual sense was particularly vivid. Growing up on the edge of Epping Forest, the once vast medieval stand of royal woods north of London, he developed an appreciation of natural forms and shapes. Morris found the trunks of the hornbeam trees rising in the forest and seen against the mass of the wood behind precise and romantic. In the family library he came across Gerard's *Herbal*, an illustrated dictionary of plants and flowers, which he read again and again. He absorbed the real and artificial images of nature, eventually using them in his designs for wallpapers, tapestries and carpets.

His sense of smell was also acute. Particular odors invariably stimulated memories of early childhood. "To this day," he once said, "when I smell a may-tree I think of going to bed by daylight." He and his sisters and brothers kept small plots to grow vegetables near the house. Years later the strong sweet smell of balm would bring to mind "very early days in the kitchen-garden" and conjure images of "the large blue plums which grew on the wall beyond the sweet-herb patch" [Mackail, I, 10]. He loved wildlife as well, giving a special place in his affections to birds of all kinds.

Morris was born the eldest son, but third of nine children, on 24 March 1834. His parents, William Morris and Emma Shelton, had grown up as neighbors in the town of Worcester, and their families were intimate with one another and distantly related. William Morris senior joined a firm of discount brokers in London when he was in his early twenties. The company, Harris, Sanderson & Harris, was new and between the Morrises and the founders there was a family connection.

Discount broking was a form of banking in which brokers provided clients cash at a discount in exchange for their agreement to repay the full amount on a fixed date. The business was highly respectable. Brokers who were able to assess the character and financial resources of their clients made a comfortable, even opulent living. Morris's father was good at his work. By the time he was thirty he was a partner in the firm, which had in the meantime simplified its name to Sanderson & Co. Soon after, he moved his young family to a commodious house, Elm House, in Walthamstow, on the outskirts of London. Walthamstow was then a pleasant village in the countryside overlooking the valley of the Lea River. A year later young William Morris was born.

Young William's very first days were inauspicious. He was a sickly infant and "had to be kept alive, his mother used to say, by calves' feet jelly and beef tea" [Mackail, I, 5]. But he soon recovered. When he was six, his father was rich enough to take the lease on Woodford Hall, a stately mansion not far from Elm House. The house was surrounded by its own park and located on the edge of Epping Forest; Palladian in style, it was largely cut off from the life of the outside world. This fostered a sense of insularity and self-sufficiency.

As a child Morris enjoyed outings to neighboring churches to take brass rubbings of medieval knights and clerics. He was greatly pleased when his father gave him (or at least allowed him to have) a small suit of armor, and he wore it while riding his pony around the park. When he was eight his father took him on a memorable visit to Canterbury to see the cathedral. He was delighted when, in the following year, the Herald's College acknowledged his father's new status as a wealthy gentleman and granted him a coat of arms, featuring three golden horseshoes with a crest of a silver horse's head.

Morris relished everything about his early days, particularly his intimate friendship with his favorite sister Emma. She was the first child, nearly four years older than he. Unlike his second sister Henrietta, Emma was charming, lovable and "specially fond" of her brother [May Morris, II, 613]. Like him she was an avid reader, and so the two spent a great deal of their time reading together. They shared a fascination for medieval romances. Often he read aloud while she listened. Years later, after he died, she remembered reading Clara Reeve's *The Old English Baron*,

> together in the rabbit warren at Woodford, poring over the enthralling pages till both were wrought up to a state of mind that made them afraid to cross the park to reach home. [Mackail, I, 8]

No doubt the romance stood out in her memory because two of the main characters are a brother and sister named William and Emma, which were also the names of their father and mother. Morris literally fell in love with his sister as they put their heads together to read.

Until the age of thirteen, Morris's childhood was the sunniest and happiest time of his life. In the autumn of 1847 however, it came to an abrupt close when his father suddenly died. In a story written several years later as a student at Oxford, the young Morris conveyed his sense of grief. The knight Amyot returns home after a long absence only to die suddenly. Walter, his young friend, recalls a poignant moment five years earlier when he and Amyot were separated after a childhood visit to a distant cathedral city, reminiscent of the trip Morris took with his father to Canterbury. "I remember how his hand left mine at last . . . and it was all like a dream that he should leave me, for we had said that we should always be together" [Morris, I, 156]. Walter's fleeting memory is interrupted by bitter reality. He finds himself standing next to Amyot's bed. As his sister leans forward and kisses him, he realizes that his friend is dead, leaving them very lonely and sad.

Several months after his father's death, Morris's mother sent him to boarding school at Marlborough College. He disliked the school and made few friends. However, he found some consolation reading books on archaeology and church architecture in the library or wandering through the neighboring countryside in search of woods and antiquities. His classmates remembered him as a "strong-looking boy, with a high colour and black curly hair, good-natured and kind, but with a fearful temper." Others recalled his curious habit of nervously kneading his fingers together for which he found an outlet in weaving string nets. "With one end of the net fastened to a desk in the big schoolroom he would work at it for hours together, his fingers moving almost automatically." He invented endless stories about knights and fairies, with which he occasionally amused his schoolmates. He was also remembered as a solitary figure who disliked football and cricket and was "fond of mooning and talking to himself, and considered a little mad by the other boys" [Mackail, I, 17].

He longed for home, though the house he loved had disappeared. His mother had given up the lease on Woodford Hall and moved to a more manageable house, Water House, not too far from Woodford, in November 1848. Still, he looked to home for comfort and waited impatiently for letters from his sister. He wrote to her at the beginning of November,

> I am sure, you must think me a great fool to be always thinking about home always, but I really can't help it I don't think it is my fault for there are such a lot of things I want to do and say, and see.

Months later he still chafed at being sent away. He wrote to her in the spring of 1849,

> I am very sorry I was not home with you at Easter, but of course that was not to be and it is no good either to you or to me to say any *horrid stale arguments* about being obliged to go to school for of course we know all about that.

Next to wishing he were at home he wanted most "to get a *tremendous* long letter from you dear Emma," as he wrote in closing one of his own [Morris Letters, I, 3-8].

Emma turned eighteen the year that her brother entered Marlborough. Three years earlier, a new curate had arrived at the church at Walthamstow where the Morrises attended services. The Reverend Joseph Oldham brought with him an enthusiasm for the Tractarians, a group of Anglican clergymen who included most notably John Henry Newman. The Tractarians wanted to reinvigorate the Church of England by creating, among other things, a sense of beauty through the revival of music and ceremony. In contrast to the evangelical community within the Church, to which the Morrises belonged, this movement was considered either a form of subversion toward Roman Catholicism or a breath of fresh air. The Tractarian (High Church or Oxford) Movement also had taken hold at Marlborough. Morris and his sister shared their appreciation of this return to medieval religious practices. "I am glad you liked the anthem on Easter Tuesday," he wrote from Marlborough. "We here had the same anthem on Monday and Tuesday as on Sunday." He "thought it was very beautiful," especially the third verse which "was sung entirely by base, not very loud but with that kind of emphasis which you would think befitting to such a subject" [Morris Letters I, 6].

While her brother was at Marlborough, Emma fell in love with the curate, and in the spring of 1850 she married him. Morris, now sixteen and apparently unaware of the courtship, was devastated. He felt that he and his sister were inseparable. Shortly after the marriage Oldham was appointed to a church in distant Derbyshire. Morris was "thus put quite out of reach of his favourite sister. He felt the separation keenly; the brother and sister had been closely intimate in all their thoughts and enthusiasms; and it was to some degree under her influence that the Church was settled on as his own destined profession" [Mackail, I, 25].

Two

Do you keep your child—love, Brother?

For a long time Morris was miserable. After Emma's marriage he continued at Marlborough, and then left for good at Christmas 1851 after a student rebellion disrupted the school. He departed with a distinct distaste for organized education. He returned home to Walthamstow to prepare for exams to enter Oxford by studying with a tutor, Frederick Guy, who taught at a nearby school. Guy, who was very interested in painting and architecture, guided him through a reading of the story of Medea, and greatly improved his knowledge of the classics.

Morris respected Guy's abilities and kept up the relationship many years later. W.H. Bliss, a fellow-pupil, remembered how strong, active and solitary Morris was at age eighteen. They played singlestick, a form of fencing with wooden swords, in which Morris was so aggressive and fierce that Bliss insisted on placing a table between them. Nearly every day they took long walks or rode on horseback through Epping Forest. When Bliss and Guy's other students took a holiday to London, Morris preferred to go to the forest by himself. He even chose to take a long ride alone to Waltham Abbey while everyone in England who could, including his fellow pupils and entire family, attended the Duke of Wellington's funeral.

Morris expected to enter Exeter College, Oxford in the autumn of 1852, but the college was over-crowded. His entry had to be postponed until the winter term.

He took and passed his matriculation exams in June 1852 sitting next to Ned Jones (later Sir Edward Burne-Jones). Jones noticed that Morris had finished his essay on Horace early and written his name across the folded page. Within the first two or three days of their first term they met again, and formed a deep and lasting friendship. Jones realized that Morris was someone special almost immediately. He said,

> From the first, I knew how different he was from all the men I had ever met. He talked with vehemence, and sometimes with violence. I never knew him languid or tired. He was slight in figure in those days; his hair was dark brown and very thick, his nose straight, his eyes hazel-coloured, his mouth exceedingly delicate and beautiful. [Mackail, I, 35]

Physically they could not have been more different. Morris was strong and handsome, Jones thin, pale and prone to sickness. Their intellectual and imaginative interests, however, were strikingly close. Both had entered the university to become churchmen and had been inspired by the Oxford Movement. Very quickly they discovered that the religious exaltation of John Henry Newman and his fellow divines had dissipated at the university that gave the movement its name. Jones later wrote,

> Gloomy disappointment and disillusion, were settling down on me in this first term's experience of Oxford. The place was languid and indifferent; scarcely anything was left to shew that it had passed through such an excited time as ended with the secession of Newman. So [Morris and I] compared our thoughts together upon these things and went angry walks together in the afternoons and sat together in the evenings reading. [Mackail, I, 35]

In their first two years they dedicated themselves to the goal of taking Holy Orders. Finding the instruction dull and uninviting, they created their own curriculum. Morris continued his habit of reading aloud and Jones proved a willing listener. They plowed through heavy fields of ecclesiastical literature. Mackail [I, 37-8] tells us that they read Neale's *History of the Eastern Church*, Milman's *Latin Christianity*, great portions of the *Acta Sanctorum*, and of the 'Tracts for the Times,' Gibbon, Sismondi, and masses of mediaeval chronicles and ecclesiastical Latin poetry.

They read Kenelm Digby's *Mores Catholici* secretly but separately, each at first afraid to acknowledge to the other the tempting lure of the Roman Church. Together they examined closely the texts of Archdeacon Wilberforce on the sacred rites of the Eucharist, Baptism and the Incarnation, and they dreamed of forming a monastery in which the brothers would practice celibacy and dedicate themselves to a spiritual life. When Wilberforce, following the example of Newman, converted to Roman Catholicism in November 1854, Morris nearly followed.

It was Jones's friends who saved them from excessive religiosity, at the same time reinforcing their drive to do right and seek truth. Jones introduced Morris to his school chums, who resided mostly in Pembroke College. William Fulford, the most senior of these men, greatly admired Tennyson's poetry and possessed "great critical insight, and extraordinary power of conversation." R.W. Dixon, the only one to ultimately take Holy Orders, became a published poet and, like Morris, was considered a possible poet laureate after the death of Tennyson. Charles Faulkner was the only one studying mathematics and not preparing for a career in the church. He won various mathematical prizes and later, like Jones, became a partner in Morris's firm, Morris, Marshall, Faulkner & Company. A year after Morris and Jones arrived, the group expanded to include Harry Macdonald, Jones's future brother-in-law, and Cormell Price.

All of these men, with the exception of Morris, came from Birmingham, and all the Birmingham men apart from Faulkner had gone to King Edward's Grammar School before entering the University. At first they thought Morris a bit backward, but they quickly realized the depth of his knowledge and the intensity of his feelings. Dixon regarded him initially,

> simply as a very pleasant boy . . . who was fond of talking, which he did in a husky shout, and fond of going down the river with Faulkner, who was a good boating man. He was very fond of sailing a boat. He was also extremely fond of singlestick, and a good fencer.

Dixon was astonished by his excitability and his "habit of beating his own head, dealing himself vigorous blows, to take it out of himself." But very soon they realized that Morris was deep.

> I remember Faulkner remarking to me, 'How Morris seems to know things, doesn't he?' And then it struck me that it was so. I observed how decisive he was: how accurate, without any effort or formality: what an extraordinary power of observation lay at the base of many of his casual or incidental remarks, and how many things he knew that were quite out of our way; as, *e.g.*, architecture. One of the first things he ever said to me was to ask me to go with him to look at Merton tower. [Mackail, I, 43-4]

All of the circle were expecting to do great things in the world. The Pembroke men were more worldly and less spiritual than Morris and Jones and more interested in secular literature, social and political issues. They engaged themselves in reading the latest works as they appeared in print. The group was particularly taken by the novels of Charles Kingsley and the poems of Tennyson, which seemed to offer a set of ideals, however vague, to follow. They all agreed that Tennyson had taken English poetry to its highest level and was unlikely to be surpassed. The group would often gather to read Tennyson, Milton and others aloud. Fulford, Dixon remembered, "had a very fine deep voice, and was a splendid reader of poetry." Although he had the least distinguished career in later life among their circle of friends, Fulford "loved moral beauty first of all things" and exerted an encouraging influence on the others, including Morris. Jones and Price were also fine readers with distinctive voices. Morris, in contrast, had "a mighty singing voice and chanted rather than read." In 1854 they started weekly readings of Shakespeare's plays in one another's rooms. They decided to draw lots for the various parts as a way to moderate the competitive spirit that developed among them. Dixon remembered "Morris's Macbeth, and his Touchstone particularly; but most of all his Claudio, in the scene with Isabel. He suddenly raised his voice to a loud and horrified cry at the word 'Isabel,' and declaimed the awful following speech, 'Aye, but to die, and go we know not where,' in the same pitch" [Mackail, I, 45, 47].

There were two new books – *The Stones of Venice* and *The Heir of Redclyffe* – that had particular and dramatic impacts on Morris and

Jones. They were already familiar with John Ruskin's *Modern Painters* and regarded him as both hero and prophet. When *The Stones of Venice* appeared in 1853 they fell on it immediately, agreeing that the chapter "Of the Nature of Gothic" represented a kind of "new gospel" [Mackail, I, 38]. Ruskin showed them that the work of the anonymous craftsmen of the Middle Ages possessed a beauty and integrity that manifested the religious feeling of the age in contrast to the soulless structures and artifacts of the new industrial era. When, years later, Morris started the Kelmscott Press he chose to print the chapter as one of his first productions. For Jones, who had earned a reputation as a drawer of fantastic creatures and caricatures at King Edward's, the book validated the spiritual nature of art and made him think of painting as a legitimate career. For Morris, who had a natural eye for line and detail, it moved him into a deeper understanding and appreciation of architecture and all its crafts. Jones began drawing from nature, visiting Bagley Wood on the outskirts of Oxford to make precise studies of flowers and foliage and in so doing finding a source of relief from the burden of theological perplexities. Morris began drawing windows, arches, gables, floriated ornaments and other architectural devices in his books and letters, going to the Bodleian library to examine the designs and color in medieval manuscripts and reading *The Builder*, an architectural newsmagazine.

About the same time Morris started to draw, he began to fashion his literary and personal experiences into poems and stories. Jones was the first of his friends to learn that he wrote poetry, though Morris was already sending poems to his sister. One important poem that he sent to Emma – and never showed to Jones – expressed his disappointment over her marriage. Brother and sister are alone when she tells him that she plans to marry. She recalls how as children they played together, how he crowned her with white lilies and promised her his "love and lealty" forever. She asks him:

> Do you keep your child-love, brother?
>   As you vowed to keep it then?
> Will you love me, if another
>   Be my lover among men?

He cries, but makes no answer. She offers a consolation:

Earth will not hold us forever,
On the earth we live not long,
When we live in heaven together
God will make our weak love strong
[Morris MS].

Exactly when Morris began to write poems and stories is unclear, but he received a strong impetus from reading Charlotte Yonge's novel *The Heir of Redclyffe,* which also appeared in 1853. The book was one of the most popular of the entire Victorian era, going through five editions in its first year and seventeen by 1868. It "exercised an extraordinary fascination" for Morris and his friends. Dixon, who thought that the novel was "unquestionably one of the finest books in the world," remembered that the hero, Sir Guy Morville, was adopted by their group "as a pattern for actual life" and more so by Morris than the others [Mackail, I, 41]. Just how and why did this Victorian classic come to have such an immediate and potent impact on him?

First, Morris was very much like Morville. Sir Guy experiences a rather cloistered childhood with few chances for making friends; he is "a very happy, joyous boy, leading an active, enterprising life, though so lonely as to occasion greater dreaminess and thoughtfulness than usual at such an age." He is handsome and strong though slightly built, and possesses penetrating, hazel eyes. He loves the outdoors, enjoys boating, prefers hunting in the forest alone, and is very fond of birds. His birthdate is 28 March; Morris was born on 24 March. He is frustrated, angry and at odds with the world. At times he suffers attacks of spontaneous violence and bites his lip until it bleeds in order to suppress his anger. He is restless and fidgets nervously with his fingers. He wants purpose in life, but is afraid that he will not find it nor achieve it if he finds it. As he declares early in the novel, "It is all failing, and resolving, and failing again" [Yonge, 49]. Before he can enter Oxford he must be tutored to compensate for a deficient education. He writes poems and reads poetry aloud with sensitivity and feeling, and he loves Sir Galahad and the stories of Malory's *Morte d'Arthur*. Though rich, he lacks a father (and a mother), worries about achieving self-control and wants guidance.

Secondly, the story provided a template for personal development, for getting from adolescence to maturity. Central to Yonge's narrative is Morville's chance discovery of the story of *Sintram*, a romance by F.H.K. la Motte Fouqué first published in German in 1814. Sintram is a callow and wayward youth who is unprepared for the responsibilities of knighthood. In the critical episode of the story he visits his mother, the beautiful and saintly Verena, who has retired to a convent. Sintram would also like to find refuge in a quiet sanctuary, but his mother tells him that he has a duty to do right in the world. Rebuffed, he sallies forth to encounter and combat evil, as suggested by Albert Durer's engraving of the Knight, Death and the Devil, printed as the frontispiece of the story. Guy Morville in turn embraces Sintram as his model and entreats his lovely cousin Amy Edmonstone to serve as his Verena. Though he eventually marries Amy, he considers her foremost as "a guide and guard whose love might arm him, soothe him and encourage him" to manly purpose [Yonge, 187, 189]. From all this Morris found in Morville "a pattern for actual life" and in *Sintram* "the germ of his own early tales" [Mackail, I, 41].

One morning in the winter term of 1855, just after they had finished breakfast, Morris read what Jones believed was his first poem. Soon after, perhaps the same evening, Dixon and Cormell Price stopped in to visit, and Jones burst forth with the news that Morris was "a big poet." Dixon remembered how they "sat down and heard Morris read his first poem, the first he had ever written in his life. It was called 'The Willow and the Red Cliff.' " The motif of the red cliff came, of course, from Charlotte Yonge's novel, but the subject was out of Morris's own experiences. Energized by Morris's forceful delivery, the poem astonished his friends. "As he read it," Dixon continued, "I felt that it was something the like of which had never been heard before. It was a thing entirely new: founded on nothing previous: perfectly original, whatever its value, and sounding truly striking and beautiful, extremely decisive and powerful in execution."

In the poem Morris presented a woman who remembers how a lover once "plighted well his troth to me," giving her a ring, which she then hung among the branches of a willow tree. She wonders if the ring is still there. At the end of the poem she holds a picture of her lover and then lets the wind waft it down to the waves below, vowing that she will join him in "the pearl-strewn cave" beneath the sea [Morris MS]. His friends expressed their enthusiasm, to which Morris responded laconically, "Well, if this is poetry, it is very easy to write" [Mackail, I, 51-2]. From then on he wrote a new poem nearly every day for several terms.

A flood of stories quickly followed the cascade of poems. In one of these tales, entitled "A Dream," he produced his own version of the Morville-Sintram story. He acknowledged at the beginning "that in some way, how I know not, I am mixed up with the strange story I am going to tell you." The story is about a young knight named Lawrence who has grown up in the house of his beautiful cousin. So it is "natural enough that they should discover as they grew up that they were in love with one another." But Lawrence is indolent and Ella must chide him to action. "Dear knight," she tells him, "truly, if you turn out a great warrior, I too shall live in fame, for I am certainly the making of your desire to fight." He responds by entering the cavern of a red cliff, "which was overhung by creepers and matted grass," as a prelude to facing a world of unspecified challenges. His entrance represents a metaphorical initiation into manhood with sexual as well as vocational implications. At the end of the story, the ashes of the cousin-lovers are buried together in a marble tomb carved with "the history of the cave in the Red Pike" [Morris, I, 160,164,175]. In this brief dream-romance Morris incorporated Emma, barely disguised as Ella, as his lady-love and guiding light.

Three

Think how long I have worshipped you, looked on the world through your eyes!

It was one thing for Morris to cast his sister in the image of a medieval lady, inspiring and guiding her man to glory, and another to live with the bitter reality that she was married and he unprepared for manhood. For several years, from 1854 when he began writing poetry until 1858 when he decided to marry, he tried to fit himself into the "pattern for actual life" that he found in Charlotte Yonge's novel. He battled with the twin difficulties of prohibited love and vocational mission.

Mindful of time's swift pace he moved rapidly on many fronts. In the summer of 1854 he made his first trip to the Continent, visiting northern France and Belgium. He was mesmerized by the art of Jan van Eyck and Hans Memling "who remained to him ever after absolute and unapproached masters of painting." He saw the churches of Amiens, Beauvais, Chartres and Rouen and was immensely impressed. He wrote an appreciative essay on Amiens, though Rouen was his favorite. Nearly forty years later, he wrote,

> I first saw the city of Rouen, then still in its outward aspect a piece of the Middle Ages: no words can tell you how its mingled beauty, history, and romance took hold on me; I can only say that, looking back on my past life, I find it was the greatest pleasure I have ever had. [Mackail, I, 48]

When he returned to Oxford he also brought with him a set of photographs of Durer's engravings.

For some time he and Jones had entertained the notion of founding a monastery, but the idea lapsed as his interests widened and he began to write. In its place, at the suggestion of Dixon, he decided to underwrite a literary magazine in which they and their friends would be the primary contributors. At first they thought to call it *The Brotherhood* but, after deciding to invite friends at Cambridge to join in the effort, they determined that the name *Oxford and Cambridge Magazine* was less monastic and more suitable. In early July 1855 Morris and Jones went to Cambridge to meet with Wilfrid Heeley, another friend from Birmingham, to discuss their plans. Morris found Cambridge a distinctly inferior place to his beloved Oxford, describing it as such "a hole of a place . . . that one feels inclined to laugh, at least I do, when I think of it" [Mackail, I, 69]. In the end the Oxford men made most of the contributions to the magazine, with Fulford and Morris making the largest individual contributions.

In May 1855 Morris and Jones saw for the first time some paintings by the Pre-Raphaelites. They had already read Ruskin's praise and were primed to be receptive. The artists, principally John Everett Millais, Holman Hunt, Ford Madox Brown and Dante Gabriel Rossetti, sought to paint in clear, bright, primary colors. Their aim was to attain the purity that existed before Raphael showed artists how to mute and even muddy their canvases. They particularly abhorred painters like Joshua Reynolds, whom they dubbed Sir Sloshua. At the house of the Director of the Clarendon Press in Oxford, Morris and Jones saw and fell in love with Rossetti's watercolor of Dante drawing the head of Beatrice. At about the same time, they came across a copy of *The Germ*, a short-lived literary magazine produced by the Pre-Raphaelite group, and were captivated by Rossetti's poem "The Blessed Damozel." Both painting and poem seemed wonderful realizations of the ideal woman who can inspire a man to greatness.

Morris felt compelled to return to France in August. The journey was meant to be a walking tour, but it began awkwardly when Morris's shoes failed him and he decided to wear a pair of gaily-colored carpet slippers. Before long he and his companions, Jones and Fulford, were traveling by train. Along the way Morris quarreled with his friends about bypassing Paris to get to Chartres. He wanted to avoid the congestion and get on to the churches and the countryside. Jones and Fulford prevailed, but Morris was so fidgety that they cut short their stay.

Once outside Paris Morris was ecstatic. He exclaimed in a letter to Price:

> O! the glories of the Churches we have seen! Crom, we have seen nine Cathedrals, and let me see how many non-Cathedral Churches; I must count them on my fingers; there, I think I have missed some but I have made out 24 all splendid Churches.

The landscape was equally beautiful. The vast fields of wheat

> mingled with the flowers, purple thistles, and blue cornflowers, and red poppies, growing together with the corn round the roots of the fruit trees, in their shadows and, sweeping up to the brows of the long low hills till they reached the sky.

And there were the trees:

> O! the trees! It was all like the country in a beautiful poem, in a beautiful Romance such as might make a background to Chaucer's Palamon and Arcite.

The squalor of civilization was offensive in contrast, and especially its industrial intrusions like the "nasty, brimstone, noisy, shrieking railway train." Truly, Morris told Price, "Railways are ABOMINATIONS; and I think I have never fairly realized this fact till this our tour" [Mackail, I, 73-7].

The trip to France was important for Morris and Jones. The confluence of various ideas and experiences over the past two years had undermined their intention to become clergymen, and the holiday carried them to a decision. On their last night in France, as they walked along the docks at Havre, they talked openly of their future and decided that they would not take Holy Orders. As soon as possible, Jones would become a painter and Morris an architect.

On his return to England Morris went to Birmingham. For three weeks in late August and September he met with Jones, Fulford, Price and Heeley and laid plans for their magazine. Price's younger sister kept a diary and recorded some of her impressions of her brother's friends. Her older sister said, "Morris is very handsome." The next day she concurred, "Morris *is* very handsome." Several days later Fulford read Tennyson's 'Palace of Art,' and "Morris also read, but he is a queer reader." On 2 September Jones and Morris "came to tea and supper. We had great fun: Morris got so excited once that he punched his own head and threw his arms about frantically." In Price's own diary, he noted that the friends "unanimously agreed that there is to be no shewing off, no quips, no sneers, no lampooning in our Magazine." A couple of days later they agreed further that the magazine would run "mainly Tales, Poetry, friendly Critiques, and social articles" [Mackail, I, 80-1]. It was during this visit to Birmingham that Jones took Morris to a local bookstore to look over a copy of Malory's *Morte d'Arthur* that he had been surreptitiously reading. Until then Morris had never seen nor read the book. He promptly bought it and Malory became a vital source for new poems.

After leaving Birmingham, Morris traveled to Clay Cross in Derbyshire and spent several days with his sister and brother-in-law before returning home to Walthamstow. In Birmingham he suggested to Price that he might not complete his degree at Oxford, and he seems to have said the same thing to Emma and to his mother. From Walthamstow he wrote to Price at the end of September to thank him for his concern and to tell him to "make your mind easy about my coming back next term, I am certainly coming back, though I should not have done so if it had not been for my Mother." Nonetheless, he was anxious to get started in architecture.

> I am too old already and there is no time to lose, I MUST make haste, it would not do for me . . . to be a lazy, aimless, useless, dreaming body all my life long.

He bent to the unpleasant task of preparing himself for his Final Schools, the comprehensive examinations required for graduation. He told Price that he was going to study "six hours a day at Livy, Ethics, &c" and begged him to "please pity me" [Mackail, I, 82-3]. Fulford, who had already graduated, agreed to coach him. Morris returned to Oxford the second week of October and on the 24th took and passed the exams, in effect compressing another year's work into two weeks. Altogether he spent two and a half years at Oxford to earn his baccalaureate degree.

Morris remained in Oxford after taking the exams and met regularly with his friends to further the work of their magazine. They hammered out a prospectus and chose a publisher, Bell and Daldy. They decided that the issues should come out monthly and run to seventy-two pages. They began to write and select the pieces for the first issue, which appeared on 1 January 1856 and included Morris's "The Story of the Unknown Church" and his poem "Winter Weather." Having settled on his change of career, Morris was also composing his thoughts before approaching his mother again.

In a long letter dated 11 November, he apologized for "speaking roughly" to her about his new plans for the future. He tried to explain that his desire to be an architect was genuine and that he no longer wished to enter the Church as a clergyman. He was worried that she might think his education at Oxford had been a waste of money, but during his three years there he had made a lot of good friends and had learned to hate all forms of sin.

More to the point, he could not imagine any kind of work other than architecture in which he had any chance of success or hope of happiness. Though his tone did not convey it, he was "pretty confident I shall succeed, and make I hope a decent architect sooner or later." He admitted that to accomplish this would require a lot of drudgery. He wrote,

> Perhaps, you think that people will laugh at me, and call me purposeless and changeable; I have no doubt they will, but I in my turn will try to shame them, God being my helper, by steadiness and hard work, [Mackail, I, 85]

He concluded by telling her that he planned to approach George Edmund Street, a leader in the field of ecclesiastical architecture and with offices in Oxford, to sign on as an apprentice.

A career in the Church had seemed eminently sensible for Morris: he had never evinced any interest in business, was high-minded, aesthetic and bookish. Serving an apprenticeship after finishing a university education struck his mother as capricious and willful. When he first spoke to her about it in October she scarcely credited him with being serious, and now the letter brought disappointment and consternation. There was, however, little that she could do other than express her anxiety. In March her son had turned twenty-one and come into his inheritance, which provided him with an annual income of about £900, a substantial sum of money for a young man. Street consented in December to take Morris on as an apprentice. They signed an agreement stipulating that he would start on 21 January.

The architect assigned him to work at his office on Beaumont Street under the supervision of Philip Webb, one of his principal assistants. Webb described Morris on his first appearance as "a slim boy like a wonderful bird just out of his shell" [Webb, 16]. Webb was only a few years older than Morris, and the two became immediate friends despite the professional difficulties that Morris experienced under his direction. On a couple of occasions during Morris's brief stint with Street, Webb went with him to his mother's house where they saddled horses to take long rides through Epping Forest.

Morris quickly learned that acquiring the basic skills of architecture entailed all the drudgery that he anticipated. Street gave him the task of copying the arch moldings from a drawing of the doorway of St. Augustine's in Canterbury, but he lacked the patience for such assignments. In exasperation he would jump up from his work and pace the floor reciting snatches of verse and at times "thumping his head resounding blows with both fists" [Webb, 16]. He knew before he began the apprenticeship that he was more interested in the emotive influence of architecture than its structure. "Even if I could say nothing else about these grand churches," he wrote in January in his essay on Amiens, "I could at least tell men how much I loved them" [Morris, I, 349].

He soon realized that he had made another mistake in his choice of career. His chagrin and apology were directly conveyed in his story "Frank's Sealed Letter." Morris, in the form of Hugh, takes a holiday from work and journeys to Epping Forest where his memory is overwhelmed by scenes from childhood. He sees himself and a young girl reading together. She is Emma, in the form of Mabel, the love of his life. We see that Hugh is greatly surprised and disappointed when he learns that Mabel has fallen in love and married another man. "O Mabel," he cries with the anguish of the jilted, "think of the things we have talked of together, thought of together!" He is no ordinary lover but a man who has adored his sweetheart since infancy.

> Think how long I have worshipped you, looked on all the world through your eyes! I loved you as soon as I saw you, even when I was a child, before I had reason almost; and my love and my reason have grown together till now. [Morris, I, 309-10]

We also learn that Hugh is failing in his work because Mabel has deserted him: "and the twenty years that I had lived with her, man and boy and little child, were gone." He is haunted by the fact that, ever since he can remember, people have told him that he had "no perseverance, no strength of will," that he was "unstable as water." Though he insists that his critics are wrong and that his will is powerful he admits that it has been crushed by love and "the wild restless passions" that go with it [Morris, I, 309-310]. This is why he is a failure.

Hugh's distress is partially relieved by the contents of Frank's sealed letter. Frank, Hugh's friend, has died and left Hugh two letters. The first instructs him to open the second only in the event of misfortune. The misfortune arises with Mabel's marriage. Broken-hearted, Hugh unseals the second letter in which Frank distinguishes between the earthly Mabel and the pure. Frank tells Hugh that the earthly Mabel is not worthy of his love but prays that he will never "forget the love you bore her in the days when you thought her noble, the noblest of all things; never cast away the gift of memory." At first Hugh is inclined to dismiss Mabel altogether, but, as he recovers from the flood of memories in the forest, he determines to heed Frank's advice. Reflecting the painful ambivalence, Morris concluded the story exclaiming, "O Mabel, if you could only have loved me! Lord, keep my memory green!" [Morris, I, 315, 325].

Four

How Sir Palomydes loved La Belle Iseult with exceeding great love out of measure

Just after Christmas 1855, as Morris prepared to enter architecture, Jones went to London to visit his aunt and find Rossetti. He had never met a real painter before, but somehow he knew that the leader of the Pre-Raphaelites was the man to see, even though he felt that he had no hope of ever knowing him. Hearing that Rossetti taught at the Working Men's College in Great Ormond Street, Jones went there one evening to attend the college's monthly meeting. Everyone was friendly and he made the acquaintance of Vernon Lushington, recently graduated from Cambridge, who knew Rossetti and offered to point him out should he appear. When Rossetti showed up, Jones was awestruck: "I saw him for the first time, his face satisfying all my worship" [Mackail, I, 101].

Lushington offered to introduce him, but Jones felt embarrassed and declined. Instead he accepted Lushington's invitation to come to a gathering of men at his rooms a few nights later. Rossetti appeared again, and Jones finally met him in early January 1856. Identifying a convert and acolyte, Rossetti invited him to visit his studio at Blackfrairs Bridge the next day. Jones stayed a long time observing the master paint a picture of "a monk copying a mouse in an illumination," and only later learned that his hero detested anyone watching him work. He did not seem surprised that Rossetti

> asked much about Morris, one or two of whose poems he knew already, and I think that was our principal subject of talk, for he seemed very much interested about him" [Mackail, I, 102].

Apparently Rossetti had seen a copy of the first number of the *Oxford and Cambridge Magazine*, which had been published only a few days earlier, containing Morris's first published story and poem. It is likely that Rossetti obtained the copy from Lushington who, evidently unknown to Jones, had worked with Wilfrid Heeley as one of the Cambridge editors of the magazine.

Rossetti read "Winter Weather" and was no doubt struck by its force. The poem is simple, but its graphic violence was uncharacteristic of Victorian poetry. The narrator rides out in full armor to encounter the foe who has insulted his lady.

> 'Twas the midnight hour,
> Deep from the tower
> Boom'd the following bell;
> Down go our lances,
> Shout for the lances!
> The last toll was his knell.
>
> There he lay, dying;
> He had, for his lying,
> A spear in his traitorous mouth;
> A false tale made he
> Of my true, true lady;
> But the spear went through his mouth
>
> [Mackail, I, 95].

The poem was unusual, even for Morris, in featuring a protagonist who is victorious.

In 1856 Gabriel Rossetti was twenty-eight years old, only a little older than Jones and Morris, yet in terms of experience and self-assurance years their senior. He was the son of Italian immigrants but thoroughly socialized as a Londoner. His father, a teacher of Italian literature, made a modest living; nonetheless, his children were well bred and literate. Rossetti's sister Christina eventually gained national prominence as a poet, and his brother William Michael became a noted literary critic. Rossetti had spent a little time studying painting with Madox Brown and Holman Hunt but was largely self-taught. He was the principal figure within the Pre-Raphaelite circle, owing more to his cheek than his painting. By the time Jones met him, however, the Pre-Raphaelite movement existed in name only for the various painters had gone their separate ways.

Once Jones moved to London in mid May to start painting under Rossetti's guidance, Morris began to spend each weekend with him in his lodgings in Chelsea. Soon the trio became constant companions. Typically Morris would arrive from Oxford on Saturday afternoon and visit an art exhibition. In the evening they would attend a play. If Rossetti found the play contemptible they would leave before it was over. Afterwards they would go to his studio in Blackfriars where they would talk into the early hours of the morning. On Sunday Rossetti would arrive in Chelsea and the friends would pass the afternoon continuing the conversation from the night before whilst reading from the *Morte d'Arthur* and listening to Morris recite his poems. On Monday morning Morris would take the train back to Oxford and return to work at Street's office.

Rossetti was generous in introducing them to his artistic friends. They soon met Madox Brown, Holman Hunt, Arthur Hughes, Thomas Woolner, and Elizabeth and Robert Browning. Jones thought Brown was a natural comic. He told a friend,

> I asked him the other day, if I wasn't very old to begin painting, and he said, 'O, no! there was a man I knew who began older; by the bye, he cut his throat the other day,' so I ask no more about men who begin late.

Morris described Hunt as a beautiful man: tall and slim with a great red beard and dark deep eyes. Morris "fell in love with" and bought his first painting from Hughes, a picture called *April Love*. It portrayed a young woman pulling away from a lover's attempt to kiss her hand, with rose petals at her feet symbolizing the transience of young love and ivy suggesting reunion in the next life. The Brownings heard one of Morris's poems and spoke very highly of it, and Rossetti thought his "Rapunzel," which first appeared in the July 1856 issue of the Magazine, was "equal to Tennyson" [Mackail, I, 106-8].

Morris in turn accepted Rossetti as a leader. He listened as Rossetti argued that any man with any poetry in him should paint, since everything lovely and true had been said in poetry, but men had scarcely begun to paint what was said in poetry. When, in July, Rossetti urged him to become an artist Morris felt compelled to try, especially since he now saw his life's work as "the embodiment of dreams in one form or another" [Mackail, I, 107]. He decided at first not to give up his architecture; he would somehow find an extra six hours a day to practice drawing. This became easier when, in August, Street moved his office to London and Morris moved in with Jones. They shared a quaint room hung with brass rubbings and Durer prints and both men went at night to life-drawing classes.

In the autumn Morris accompanied Street on a trip to look at churches in the Low Countries, and took the opportunity to re-visit the paintings of van Eyck. Inspired by the artist's motto "Als ich kanne" (If I can), he came back "fired with new enthusiasm for painting" [Mackail, I, 107]. Shortly after the trip he tendered his resignation. When he finally found the nerve to tell his mother the news came as a shock, made all the worse because "with characteristic vehemence, he did not prepare her mind for it, but announced it with a nervous suddenness" [Mackail, I, 111]. There was, in fact, very little he could say. He had already used all of his best arguments in explaining his decision to give up the ministry to become an architect. Concerned by her son's lack of stability Mrs. Morris also blamed Jones, who had unwittingly accompanied Morris to his mother's house.

Mrs. Morris had reason to worry. The decision to trade architecture for painting "had an unsettling, and for a time, almost a disastrous effect" on her son [Mackail, I, 111]. During the two years in which he worked at painting he was moody and irritable; his mind was haunted by ridicule and failure. In "Lindenborg Pool," a story that came out in September 1856, he imagined himself as a priest called to administer the last rites to a dying man. It is midnight sometime in the thirteenth century when he enters a dark mansion to do his duty. What he encounters is a mad house where a crowd of people swirls about him laughing and jabbering maniacally. He finds the bed of the dying man, but lifting the sacrament, he is battered by a thunderclap of laughter. The man is in fact a huge swine that tears the Holy Thing from his hand, scoring him with its sharp tusk. As the priest stands bleeding and confused, the intolerable laughter rises to a shriek and hundreds of faces wheel around him. Women loosen their long hair, hem him in with interlaced arms and thrust "their horribly-grinning unsexed faces" into his [Morris, I, 252]. The holy man is overwhelmed with disgust and feels himself losing his sanity.

September also saw the appearance of the first installment of his story "The Hollow Land" with the second part following in October. Here too Morris invented a tale of defeat and retreat, which he divided into three sections: "Struggling in the World," "Failing in the World," and "Leaving the World." The hero, Florian of the House of the Lilies, struggles to defend himself against the forces of Red Harald. After a long engagement Florian finally succumbs. He is literally driven underground as the enemy, "holding their long spears out," force him back until the ground gives way beneath his feet and he falls in a cloud of dust and dirt through a widening crack in the turf. As he falls he thinks he is descending into hell, but then realizes that he is in a very special place, called the Hollow Land, hidden beneath the earth. Here he finds his true love, her name is Margaret and she comes from the far distant past. Gazing deeply into her eyes he sees his face reflected "seen in that way and no other, long and long and long ago" [Morris, I, 290]. As the story ends, Florian and Margaret open a set of golden gates and enter a great space filled with flowers. No one is there to deny them.

Once Morris quit Street's office to draw and paint full-time, there was no longer sufficient space in Jones's tiny lodging to serve both as studio and living quarters for two artists. They learned that the rooms in Red Lion Square that Rossetti and Walter Deverell had shared in the early days of the Pre-Raphaelite Movement were available. At Rossetti's urging, they leased the space in November. The rooms were on the first floor, and included a large sitting room overlooking the square and two bedrooms, a medium-sized one and a smaller one in the rear. The sitting room that served as their studio had a northern exposure, and the window had been altered to reach the ceiling and provide more light. They shared the house with a family of feather-dressers named Fauconnier who carried on their business below.

The apartment was short of furniture, so Morris set about the job of designing some. He thus embarked on a task that, though it distracted him from painting, laid the groundwork for his eventual career. He drew up some rough plans, found a local carpenter and commissioned the building of several big pieces. The first was a large round table "as firm, and as heavy, as a rock." Next came a pair of huge chairs "such as Barbarossa might have sat in" [Mackail, I, 113]. Then Morris designed a large settle with a long seat and a set of cupboards above. Somehow the carpenter misunderstood the measurements and made the piece bigger than Morris intended. Jones and Morris were both out when the settle arrived. When they returned they found their staircase clogged as the carpenter's men struggled to make delivery. After a lot of shouting and recriminations the men pushed the piece of furniture into the apartment, and their studio suddenly became a third smaller.

They worried about what Rossetti would think. When their leader arrived, he "laughed, but approved" [Mackail, I, 113]. In fact he was so taken by the project that he immediately set about making designs to be painted on the cupboard doors and sides of the settle. Over the ensuing weeks the friends painted pictures of the meeting of Dante and Beatrice in Florence and their meeting in Paradise. On the backs of the two chairs they painted scenes drawn from two of Morris's poems: the prince kissing Guendolen's long golden hair as she stands captive in the witch's tower from "Rapunzel," and the knight's arming from "Sir Galahad: a Christmas Mystery." Morris also commissioned the production of a wardrobe that Jones painted with a scene from "The Prioress's Tale" from Chaucer's *The Canterbury Tales.*

As much as Jones and Morris deferred to his authority, Rossetti enjoyed their company. To a friend, the painter William Bell Scott, he wrote warmly about his new companions in early 1857. He was impressed that, despite having studied at Oxford, they had decided to shun the usual careers open to university graduates and become artists. He thought that they showed real promise.

> Jones's designs are marvels of finish and imaginative detail, unequaled by anything unless perhaps Albert Durer's finest works, and Morris, though without practice as yet, has no less power, I fancy. [Rossetti Letters, I, 319]

Before Morris himself realized it, Rossetti discerned that Morris's real talent lay in his facility in pattern designs. "In all illumination and work of that kind," he wrote just before Christmas 1856, "he is quite unrivaled by anything modern that I know" [Mackail, I, 114]. He was happy to have Morris and Jones as friends because they were talented, original and full of enthusiasm.

At Red Lion Square Morris and Jones hired a young woman named Mary Nicholson to serve as their cook and housekeeper. She was a remarkable character whom they dubbed Red Lion Mary. She was surprisingly literate, had a good knowledge of poetry and, between cooking, mending and cleaning, would read to them from the newspaper while they worked at their art. Mary often stood behind them and watched as they painted. Though rather homely and a bit short she wanted very much to be used as a model and offered to stand on a stool if that would help. Jones was charmed by her interest and drew her portrait, which he gave her when she married. Mary found Morris outrageous and helpless, but fortunately she was endowed with good humor. "Though he was so short-tempered," she once said, "I seemed so necessary to him at all times, and felt myself his Man Friday" [GBJ, I, 171]. Once however she was so annoyed that she set his watch an hour ahead so that he left early and had an extra long wait for a train to Oxford.

Throughout the spring of 1857 Morris worked hard at drawing and painting, despite the many diversions that he created for himself. He struggled fruitlessly to master the human figure, and this was the source of much of his irritability. After a year of practice he had accomplished little. In June he was trying to paint "Sir Tristram after his Illness in the Garden of King Mark's Palace, recognized by the Dog he had given to Iseult," a scene from the *Morte d'Arthur*. Rossetti remained optimistic, reporting to William Bell Scott that, although "Morris has as yet done nothing in art," he was painting his first picture, that of Sir Tristram. "It is being done all from nature of course, and I believe will turn out capitally." Morris never completed the work. In contrast, Rossetti continued,

> his chum Jones, who is by far the most advanced of the two, is getting commissions fast, and has done some wonderful cartoons in colour for stained glass, which would delight the soul of you" [Rossetti Letters, I, 325].

In June Rossetti asked Jones to join him on a trip to Oxford to pay a call on Benjamin Woodward. Jones was too busy so Morris went instead. Woodward, an architect and friend of Rossetti, had received a commission to build a new museum at the university and had invited Rossetti to offer some designs for a mural commemorating the life and work of Sir Isaac Newton. Rossetti found the subject unappealing but, on seeing the new hall that Woodward was also building for the debating union, proposed to paint some of its walls with scenes from the *Morte d'Arthur.* An understanding was reached among Woodward, Rossetti and the building committee of the Union that Rossetti would find ten painters who would volunteer their time and talent to paint one wall each, and the Union would cover the cost of their materials and living expenses.

Rossetti quickly assembled a crew of muralists that included Morris, Jones, Arthur Hughes, Hungerford Pollen, Spencer Stanhope, Val Prinsep and himself. Prinsep, who was nineteen years old and had just begun to study painting, pleaded inexperience. He relented, however, when Rossetti told him,

> Nonsense, there's a man I know who has never painted anything – his name is Morris – he has undertaken one of the panels and he will do something very good you may depend – so you had better come. [GBJ, I, 159]

He was unable to persuade three of his older and more experienced friends. William Bell Scott, Holman Hunt and Madox Brown declined to join what came to be remembered as the Jolly Campaign.

Morris, Rossetti and Jones returned to Oxford in August to begin work, and the others turned up soon after. Val Prinsep, who was a big man ("six feet one, 15 stone, not fat, well-built, hair like finest wire, short, curly and seamless,") and able to pick up Jones and carry him up a ladder, knew Rossetti and Jones, but had never met Morris before the expedition to Oxford. When they were finally introduced one evening, Prinsep was amazed. Rossetti asked Morris to read some of his poems; Morris demurred, saying that Rossetti had heard them all. "Never mind," Rossetti replied, "here's Prinsep who has never heard them, and besides, they are devilish good." With his melancholy eyes fixed on the reader Rossetti curled up on the sofa, Jones worked silently at a pen-and-ink drawing and Morris read in a singsong chant from his collection, all the while "jiggling about nervously with his watch chain." Afterwards Prinsep returned to his room with his "brain in a whirl" [GBJ, I, 162].

Morris chose for his mural a design with a familiar theme: "How Sir Palomydes loved La Belle Iseult with exceeding great love out of measure, and how she loved not him again but rather Sir Tristram" [Mackail, I, 119]. Eager to begin Morris was also the first to finish. Unable to get his figures right he covered all but the heads with a profusion of sunflowers. Rossetti suggested that he might help another of the painters who was having difficulties by covering his figures with a mass of scarlet runners. Morris ignored the dig and undertook to paint the wooden ceiling as Hungerford Pollen had done a few years earlier in the chapel of Merton College. Rossetti painted "Sir Lancelot's Vision of the Sangreal" and Jones did "The Death of Merlin." Stanhope, who was assigned the adjacent wall, was impressed with Jones's devotion to his painting. Stanhope had started later than the others, and because Jones painted carefully and slowly, the two worked side by side for some weeks after the others had finished. For Jones the reward for his dedication was several reviews that appeared in the press early in the new year in which he received favorable mention for his work.

The debating society did not see the work until they assembled at the beginning of the new school year. When they did so however there were some members who were not pleased with the project. They complained that the work had not been properly authorized and that costs had exceeded expectations. The paintings were also extremely difficult to see. The walls that Rossetti chose to paint were the ten spaces between the windows at the top of the bookshelves on the upper gallery of the debating hall. Nearly twenty feet from the debating hall floor they could only be seen at a distance and at a sharp angle. Light from the windows further obscured the paintings. The artists moreover, who should have known better, did not properly prepare the walls for mural work and the color began to fade soon after.

The painters however had a good time. Morris, who had begun to put on weight, was the object of much of their amusement. Rossetti and Jones drew a number of caricatures showing him in different guises. One cartoon showed him suddenly discovering that he was now fat, another denying that anything about him had changed except the length of his hair and another angrily twirling his watch chain. As the most handsome of the crew he often posed for the heads of the heroes. In search of authenticity he found a blacksmith who made him a helmet and coat of mail. When he returned from the forge with the helmet he tried it on and became furious when he couldn't make the visor go up or down. From his perch high above the floor of the debating hall Jones watched him "embedded in iron, dancing with rage and roaring inside" [Mackail, I, 121]. When the smith delivered the coat of mail Morris was so pleased that he wore it to dinner. Jones thought he looked splendid.

Begun in August, work on the murals continued into the autumn. This allowed Morris and Jones to see their friends who were still at the university. During the day Price, Faulkner and others often stopped by the hall to check on the progress of the frescoes. In the evening the group usually had dinner together and played cards afterwards. In his diary Price recorded some of these gatherings. On the evening of 30 October, Morris read his poem "The Defence of Guenevere" to a rapt audience of twelve. Price pronounced the poem "very grand." On the following night they played whist together, Rossetti and Price against Faulkner and Morris. Madox Brown turned up, and Rossetti declared that Morris "had the greatest capacity for producing and annexing dirt of any man he ever met with" [Mackail, I, 126-7]. On the evening of 1 November, Morris and Jones were introduced for the first time to Algernon Swinburne who had entered Oxford in the previous January.

Morris finished his decoration of the roof in early November, but stayed in Oxford as the others completed their paintings. During this time he continued to work at other crafts besides drawing and painting. He made designs for stained-glass windows, began some of his first experiments in weaving and embroidery, carved a block of stone into a capital of birds in foliage and tried making a clay head of Price. The last was never finished because "whenever Morris grew impatient he flew at it and smashed it up." On several other occasions he lost his temper. At dinner one evening Prinsep said something that offended him. Instead of an outburst of rage he bottled up his anger and merely bit into his fork, which he "crushed and twisted about almost beyond recognition" [Mackail, I, 129]. In October he went to Manchester to visit Dixon and see the Art Treasures Exhibition. When it was time to leave he and Dixon misread the train schedule, which forced Morris to stay an extra day. When he realized the mistake Morris let out a fearful shout and became "translated." His fit lasted all the way back to Dixon's: "it then vanished in a moment; he was as calm as if it had never been, and began painting in water-colours" [Mackail, I, 115]. As he often did when he felt miserable, he slipped into his imagination to find peace. He called the painting – the only watercolor he is known to have done – "The Soldan's Daughter in the Palace of Glass."

Five

There comes no sleep nor any love; Ah me! I shiver with delight

Morris gathered, selected and then published in March 1858 his poems in a slim volume entitled *The Defence of Guenevere and Other Poems*. He dedicated the work to his friend Dante Gabriel Rossetti. The collection represented some of the finest poetry of the Victorian age and certainly the best that Morris was ever to write. The poems give sharp, swift and detailed realizations of specific, mostly tragic, events. Swinburne, a fine poet and acute critic, saw that the poems directly reflected Morris's mind: "Upon no piece of work in the world was the impress of native character ever more distinctly stamped, more deeply branded" [Mackail, I, 131]. The poems form a poignant record of a mind concentrated on defeat and sexual frustration.

With few exceptions he wrote of heroes who fail in one way or another. In "Sir Peter Harpdon's End" the commander is forced to surrender the castle he defends and then is hanged. His lady Alice receives the news and knows no minstrel will sing a loser's praise:

> Yea, some men sing, what is it then they sing?
> Eh? Launcelot, and love and fate and death;
> They ought to sing of him who was as wight
> As Launcelot or Wade, and yet avail'd
> Just nothing, but to fail and fail and fail,
> And so at last to die and leave me here,
> Alone and wretched; yea, perhaps they will,
> When many years are past, make song of us;

God help me, though, truly I never thought
That I should make a story in this way [Morris, I, 60].

In "The Haystack in the Floods" Sir Robert rescues his lady Jehane from Godmar's castle only to be caught in the countryside. Godmar offers Jehane a deal: yield her body within the hour in exchange for Robert's life. She learns that the price of purity is quick and ugly when she says, "I will not."

With a start
Up Godmar rose, thrust them apart;
From Robert's throat he loosed the bands
Of silk and mail; with empty hands
Held out, she stood and gazed, and saw
The long bright blade without a flaw
Glide out from Godmar's sheath, his hand
In Robert's hair; she saw him bend
Back Robert's head; she saw him send
The thin steel down; the blow told well,
Right backward the knight Robert fell,
And moaned as dogs do, being half dead,
Unwitting, as I deem: so then
Godmar turn'd grinning to his men,
Who ran, some five or six, and beat
His head to pieces at their feet [Morris, I, 128].

Some of his poems are more subtle. In "The Chapel in Lyoness" Ozana le cure Hardy is a chaste knight of pure heart, but lies dying in the church-aisle with little to show for his life:

SIR OZANA
All day long and every day,
From Christmas-Eve to Whit-Sunday,
Within that Chapel-aisle I lay,
And no man came a-near.

Naked to the waist was I,
And deep within my breast did lie,
Though no man any blood could spy,
The truncheon of a spear . . . .

Sometimes strange thoughts pass through my head;
Not like a tomb in this my bed,
Yet oft I think that I am dead;
    That round my tomb is writ:

"Ozana of the hardy heart,
Knight of the Table Round,
Pray for his soul, lords, of your part;
    A true knight he was found."
    Ah! me, I cannot fathom it.
        He sleeps.

Galahad watches over him all day and every day until his madness and his life pass away.

There comes no sleep nor any love;
Ah me! I shiver with delight.

I am so weak I cannot move;
    God move me to thee, dear, to-night!
Christ help! I have but little wit:
My life went wrong; I see it writ.

"Ozana of the hardy heart,
    Knight of the Table Round,
Pray for his soul, lords, on your part;
    A good knight he was found."
Now I begin to fathom it.
        He dies

[Morris, I, 31-3].

Morris leaves his reader to wonder what Ozana finally fathoms. Is the poem simply about a good but vanquished man dying apart from his loved one? Does shivering with delight half naked in bed, with a bloodless shaft protruding suggest a young man sexually aroused? No one can know for sure, but poetry is designed to be suggestive.

Galahad also conveyed Morris's inner thoughts. "Sir Galahad: a Christmas Mystery" begins quietly:

It is the longest night in all the year,
Near on the day when the Lord Christ was born;
Six hours ago I came and sat down here,
And ponder'd sadly, wearied and forlorn.

The winter wind that pass'd the chapel door,
Sang out a moody tune, that went right well
With mine own thoughts . . .

Galahad questions a fruitless quest:

. . .. [with] half-shut eyes upon the ground,
I thought: O Galahad! the days go by,
Stop and cast up now that which you have found,
So sorely you have wrought and painfully.

Night after night your horse treads down alone
The sere damp fern, night after night you sit
Holding the bridle like a man of stone,
Dismal, unfriended, what thing comes of it?

Galahad's search for the Sangreal, the holy vessel containing Christ's blood, is going badly and there is no love to console him. Launcelot can ride forth armed with memories of Guenevere. Even Palomydes, denied real love like Galahad, is fortified by an idealization of Iseult:

And what if Palomydes also ride,
And over many a mountain and bare heath
Follow the questing beast with none beside?
Is he not able still to hold his breath

With thoughts of Iseult? doth he not grow pale
With weary striving, to seem best of all
To her, "as she is best," he saith? to fail
Is nothing to him, he can never fall.

For unto such a man love-sorrow is
So dear a thing unto his constant heart,
That even if he never win one kiss
Or touch from Iseult, it will never part.

Six

As for me, I choke and grow quite faint to see My lady moving graciously

During the Jolly Campaign the painters liked to attend the theatre. One evening in Oxford, Jones and Rossetti discovered two attractive young women, not on the stage, but in the audience sitting right behind them. They were sisters, Bessie and Janey, and lived in Holywell Street. Their father, Robert Burden, worked for Symonds's livery stable. Rossetti felt Bessie was very pretty but thought Janey a real "stunner" because she was tall and slender with a long neck and an abundance of black and crinkled hair. She was also pleasant, relaxed and surprisingly literate. Morris met her shortly after and also found her attractive.

In the late autumn, as the work on the Union hall came to an end, Rossetti returned to London leaving his wall unfinished. This premature return was caused, in part, because his companion and future wife Elizabeth Siddal was ill again. Lizzie Siddal, as her friends called her, had beautiful red-gold hair and great green eyes. She worked in a shop, painted in watercolors, modeled for Rossetti and was his Blessed Damozel. Jones and the other painters also returned home when their work was done, but Morris stayed and courted Janey Burden. Before long he had incorporated her into his poetry. In "In Praise of My Lady," one of the last poems to be added to *The Defence of Guenevere* before it was sent to press, he described her with tenderness and reverence:

> My lady seems of ivory
> Forehead, straight nose, and cheeks that be
> Hallow'd a little mournfully,
> *Beata mea Domina!*

Her forehead, overshadow'd much
By bows of hair, has a wave such
As God was good to make for me.
Beata mea Domina!

Not greatly long my lady's hair,
Nor yet with yellow colour fair,
But thick and crisped wonderfully:
Beata mea Domina! . . ..

Her great eyes, standing far apart,
Draw up some memory from her heart,
And gaze out very mournfully;
– Beata mea Domina! –

So beautiful and kind they are,
But most times looking out afar,
Waiting for something, not for me.
Beata mea Domina! . . .

All men that see her any time,
I charge you straightly in this rhyme,
What, and wherever you may be,
– Beata mea Domina! –

To kneel before her; as for me,
I choke and grow quite faint to see
My lady moving graciously.
Beata mea Domina!

[Morris, I, 141-3]

They spent long hours together as he read to her and she sat for him. Soon they were falling in love. By February 1858 it was apparent that they would marry. Swinburne, still a student at Oxford, remarked, "The idea of his marrying her is insane. To kiss her feet is the utmost man should dream of doing" [Swinburne Letters, I, 18].

Morris's painting however was not going well at all. He was working on several canvases; one was sold with Rossetti's help but others disappeared. He started a portrait of Janey Burden as Guenevere but was "hating the brute" the entire time [Webb, 34]. Constantly frustrated with his efforts his dream of making a career as an artist disintegrated. In its place he began to envisage a different future:

> The external impulse under which he had become a painter had exhausted its force. A new kind of life opened out vaguely before him, in which that 'small Palace of Art of my own,' long ago recognized by him as one of his besetting dreams, was now peopled with the forms of wife and children, and contracted to the limits of some actual home. [Mackail, I, 137]

Until now his vision of a quiet retreat removed from the turmoil of the real world was the safe haven that he called the Hollow Land where he found his love from long ago. How or even whether Morris told his mother that he would marry, much less that he would not continue as a painter, no one knows. We can only surmise that he said very little, because there was nothing sensible that he could say. He had begun three different careers (the ministry, architecture and painting), been sure that each was the right one, and given them all up after a short period of time. With an inheritance but without income from his own efforts and none in sight, he planned to take as his wife a pleasant, striking-looking girl from the working class, herself without social connections and financial resources. Equally painful was his knowing that marriage meant breaking faith with his childhood pledge of "love and lealty" to his sister.

In the year or so before his marriage he was more restless and out of sorts than usual. He stayed much of the time in Oxford, but also returned from time to time to Red Lion Square. His connection with Jones and Rossetti slipped. Rossetti was preoccupied with his own work and Miss Siddal's health. Jones was ill much of the time himself and often stayed with friends who were willing to give him care. In the spring of 1858 Morris's book of poems appeared but received little notice. In the summer he took off for France with Webb and Faulkner. He was agitated the entire trip. Webb recalled,

> At Amiens, on the Tower of the Cathedral, Morris upset his sovereigns from the satchel in which he carried them. I had to stop them from running out of the gargoyles by putting my foot on them.

A few minutes later he settled down to sketch the choir while Webb and Faulkner explored the galleries above. "Looking down, we saw him have a struggle with himself and suddenly go away – he had upset the ink bottle all over his drawing." Before they left, he had ordered a boat shipped over from Oxford to travel down the Seine. When the boat arrived in Paris with a hole in one side, he was "transported," and, flailing about in rage, scraped the skin from his hand against the stones at the base of one of the bridges. When he regained control, he seemed totally unaware of what had happened, even though "the bridges were lined with people" who wondered at the explosion [Webb, 23-5].

The strain of failing at work and reneging on pure love was too much. He suffered an emotional breakdown.

> In the late autumn there are references to an illness, cheerfully attributed by his friends to his eating and drinking too much, or rather to his being quite careless (as he remained always) of what he ate and drank. In October he was in France again, "to buy old manuscripts and armour and ironwork and enamel." The instability which he found, or thought he found, in his own character became for a time acute. The overstrain of the crowded years through which he had been passing, with all their inward revolutions, all their pangs of growth and fevers of imagination, had left him, like some lover in one of his own poems, languid and subject to strange fluctuations of mood. [Mackail, I, 137]

Nonetheless, William Morris and Jane Burden were married in the spring of 1859, and remained happily married for about seven years. Enjoying a contentment that he had not experienced since childhood, he abandoned painting, ceased writing poems and stories, and produced a family instead. The wedding took place on 26 April in a church renovated by George Street in Oxford. Faulkner served as best man and Dixon conducted the ceremony, calling the bridegroom and bride, though warned against making the mistake, "William and Mary," to everyone's amusement. Jones attended but Rossetti was unable to come. The Burdens were there, but apparently none of the Morrises, reflecting perhaps ignorance of the event or a disinclination to countenance a bad match.

After the wedding the newlyweds traveled to Europe, touring Belgium and northern France. On their return they took furnished rooms at 41 Great Ormond Street to await the completion of their dream house. It was at Great Ormond Street that Georgie MacDonald, soon to marry Ned Jones, met Janey Morris. Georgie, a pretty, intelligent, petite young woman, was amazed by Janey's extraordinary beauty. She recalled,

> There, Edward took me one evening to see Mrs. Morris for the first time, and never shall I forget it – literally I dreamed of her again in the night. [GBJ, I, 195]

The two young women, then nineteen-year olds, immediately became close friends. Following the Morris's lead, Lizzie Siddal and Rossetti, and then Georgie and Ned Jones were married in the ensuing spring, 1860. In the summer Janey and Morris moved into their new home.

It was designed by Webb who conceived it in a Gothic style, made from red brick, featuring steep red-tiled roofs. It was built in the countryside in an old apple orchard near Bexley Heath about ten miles from central London, south of the Thames. Once settled, Morris set about making Red House into a palace of art. He commissioned Jones to decorate the interior, and invited Rossetti and Faulkner to help. They chose designs from medieval romances and classical tales, his father's coat of arms, and Van Eyck's motto "If I can." The Joneses stayed for several weeks to do the work. Georgie Jones recalled their first

> arrival at Abbey Wood Station, a country place in those days, where a thin fresh air full of sweet smells met us as we walked down the platform, and outside was the wagonette sent from Red House to meet us; then a pull up the hill and a swinging drive of three miles of winding road on the higher land until, passing 'Hog's Hole' on the left, we stopped at our friends' gate. I think Morris must have brought us down from town himself, for I can see the tall figure of a girl standing alone in the porch to receive us.[GBJ, I, 208]

She remembered Red House as an enchanted and happy place. There were weekend gatherings, and a carefree and light-hearted atmosphere with endless games and laughter. She wrote,

> A fragment of one of these games, remains in my memory, and I see that Edward, leaving the door open behind him, has slipped into an unlighted room and disappeared into its black depths for so long that Mrs. Morris, who is the seeker, grows almost terrified. I see her tall figure and her beautiful face as she creeps slowly nearer and nearer to the room where she feels sure he must be, and at last I hear her startled cry and his peal of laughter as he burst from his hiding-place. . . .
>
> Oh, how happy we were, Janey and I, busy in the morning with needlework or wood-engraving, and in the afternoon driving to explore the country round by the help of a map of Kent; we went to Crays one day and to Chislehurst Common another, finding some fresh pleasure everywhere and bringing back tales of our adventures to amuse the men we had left working at home. . . .
>
> One morning as Janey and I sat sewing (she was an exquisite needlewoman) I saw in her basket a strange garment, fine, small, and shapeless – a little shirt for him or her – and looking at my friend's face I knew that she had been happy when she made it. [GBJ, I, 213]

In January 1861 Jane Alice Morris was born; in the following year Janey gave birth to a second daughter, whom they named Mary. Within the family the girls were known as Jenny and May.

The year 1861 also saw the conception of a new business. Brown and Rossetti convinced five of their friends – Morris, Jones, Webb, Faulkner and Peter Paul Marshall, an engineering friend of Brown's – to join with them to form a company that would design and manufacture decorative arts, in particular wall coverings, furniture, carvings, metal work and stained glass. They called the business Morris, Marshall, Faulkner and Co. It is likely that the name was chosen because the four silent partners were acknowledged artists with independent reputations while the three named partners were not. Morris came first because he supplied the cash to get the business going. Informally they referred to themselves as the Firm.

The partners appointed Morris general manager at £150 a year. They rented space for an office and workshop at 8 Red Lion Square, only a few houses down from where Morris and Jones had lived a few years earlier. They created samples of their product lines that they displayed at the International Exhibition in 1862. They did not intend to sell directly to the general public, but hoped to distribute their wares through jobbers, decorators and architects. Their first important customer was George Street's firm (where Webb and Morris used to work), which specialized in church renovation. Street needed a supply of high quality stained glass for replacements. Morris found George Campfield, an experienced stained glassmaker, and hired him as foreman. All of the partners, with the exception of Faulkner, supplied some designs. Jones however supplied the most and by far the best.

At first the business was as much a social club as a commercial enterprise. All the partners found their main source of income in their professional careers or, as in the case of Morris, in inherited wealth. Though they all hoped the business would prosper, none was counting on major dividends anytime soon. At best they might earn small commissions from supplying designs. Business meetings therefore were often more about having a good time than plotting corporate strategy. The Firm, Faulkner wrote to Price in April 1862,

> has meetings once or twice a fortnight, which have rather the character of a meeting of the 'Jolly Masons' or the jolly something elses than of a meeting to discuss business. Beginning at 8 or 9 p.m. they open with the relation of anecdotes which have been culled by members of the firm since the last meeting – this store being exhausted, Topsy [Morris] and Brown will perhaps discuss the relative merits of the art of the thirteenth and fifteenth century, and then perhaps after a few more anecdotes business matters will come up about 10 or 11 o'clock and be furiously discussed till 12, 1, or 2. [Mackail, I, 157]

Morris did not invent the Firm, but from the beginning it meant more to him than it did to the others. It became his occupation. He loved the work, and he loved his home. But the two were far apart. The daily journey between Red Lion Square and Red House was long and wearisome, especially as he was missing the last train from London now and again. In 1864 he put forward the idea of moving the Firm to Bexley Heath. He proposed to add a wing to Red House to accommodate the Joneses. When Ned and Georgie embraced the plan, he asked George Campfield to move to Bexley Heath as well. His palace of art would bring the joys of home and work together under one roof in a beautiful setting far from a hectic world. He would have a kind of earthly paradise south of London.

Seven

She stayed me, and cried "Brother!" our lips met

Morris's grand scheme was struck down by illness. In September 1864 the Morrises, Joneses and Faulkners went to Littlehampton to enjoy the seaside. Their vacation was ruined by an outbreak of scarlet fever. The Jones's young son became infected and soon recovered, but on returning to London Georgie became dangerously ill and remained so for a long while. Then, in the autumn, Morris succumbed to a crippling attack of rheumatic fever. For some weeks he was bed-ridden. Jones himself was not in the best health and worried about his wife, his friend and the wisdom of uprooting himself from the work he knew for the uncertainty of the countryside. He wrote to Morris to say that he had changed his mind. He and Georgie would not move to Bexely Heath after all.

Morris was crushed. He started a letter in reply in late November but burned it because "it read so dismal." A few days later he wrote a second. He began,

> As to our palace of Art, I confess your letter was a blow to me at first, though hardly an unexpected one – in short I cried; but I have got over it now . . . I am only 30 years old, I shan't always have the rheumatism, and we shall have a lot of jolly years of invention and lustre plates together I hope. [Morris Letters, I, 38]

Sick in bed, disappointed and anxious he reflected on his life, all one score years and ten. With great regret, he decided to give up Red House in which "he had enjoyed five years of almost unclouded happiness, and go back to live in London" [Mackail, I, 164]. A few years later he looked back on this event as an awakening, describing himself as a man who had shelved his earlier ambitions to enjoy the sweet pleasures of domesticity:

> At first indeed death seemed so far away,
> So sweet in our new home was every day,
> That we forgot death like the most of men
> Who cannot count the threescore years and ten;
> Yet we grew fearful as the time drew on,
> And needs must think of all we might have won,
> Yea, by so much the happier that we were
> By just so much increased on us our fear,
> And those old times of our past misery
> Seemed not so evil as the days went by
> Faster and faster with the years' increase,
> For loss of youth to us was loss of peace.
>
> [Morris, III, 59]

He saw that time was passing him by and the old goals of conquest and achievement should not be sacrificed to comfort and happiness.

Morris sold Red House in 1865 and took a long-term lease on a large residence in Queen Square, once a fashionable address but now a seedy backwater. The ground level was given over to workshops for the Firm, and he, Janey and their little girls moved into the upper floors. In the spring Rossetti convinced William Cowper, the First Commissioner of Public Works, to award the Firm several contracts, including a highly visible project to re-decorate one of the principal rooms in St. James's Palace. The outlook for Morris, Marshall, Faulkner & Co. brightened significantly. Since the appearance of his book of poems in 1858 Morris had written nothing of consequence. As he threw himself into delivering the newly won decorating jobs he also embarked on an intensive writing project, the poetic re-telling of ancient legends in a multi-volume series to be called *The Earthly Paradise.* So, the man who had been content to live comfortably, even playfully, in a charming country retreat became serious. Now a craftsman, no longer a country gentleman, he lived above the shop, sweated and savored a new life.

At Queen Square he began working day and night. During the day he met the rising tide of new orders for the Firm; in the evening he wrote late into the night, sometimes all night. Once started, he worked swiftly. The first tale took on a life of its own and came out as a separate volume in June 1867 as *The Life and Death of Jason*. Jason, both the character and the book, expressed an exuberant sense of new departures, manly adventures and great conquests. Homes, wives, children and domestic cares are left behind as men gather to go out in search of the Golden Fleece. The press greeted *Jason* widely and favorably, in contrast to their reaction to Morris's earlier book of poems. Morris was elated and looked forward to producing further volumes.

For Janey Morris the new departure brought a bitter turn. Georgie Jones remembered that the social life of the set initially continued, as before, to center on the Morris household, but the situation soon changed as the cheerful and buoyant hostess began to suffer a new, but chronic and undefined ailment. She wrote,

> A pleasant custom soon began of our dining in Queen Square once a week to meet other members of the Firm, and in these evenings the merriment of our youth was revived for a time, but Janey was now so much out of health that I fear her share of the entertainments was more fatigue than pleasure, and gradually they came to an end. The men never ceased to meet regularly, though, at one house or the other. [GBJ, I, 299]

Absorbed in his work, unavailable day and night, careless of domestic affairs and bolstered by male support Morris distanced himself from his wife. In telling the story of Jason's adventures, he recorded what was taking place in his own life.

In the most intimate and touching scene in the story he showed Jason lying awake while Medea sleeps at his side. He looks at her breathing easily, her fingers relaxed, and turns away in pain, wishing he were dead. His love has changed and he is tortured by guilt. But when day arrives he is up and away to join the rowdy world of men, seeking new conquests and searching for Cleonae, his new/old love. Medea is wise to the fact that he no longer loves her as he did. The more affectionate she becomes the more he shrinks away:

. . . when darksome night is well-nigh done,
And earth is waiting silent for the sun;
Then would he turn about his mate to see,
From lips half open breathing peacefully;
And open, listless, the fair fingers laid,
That unto him had brought such mighty aid.
Then groaning from her would he turn away,
And wish he might not see another day,
For certainly his wretched soul he knew,
And of the cruel God his heart that drew.
But when the bright day had come round again,
With noise of men, came foolish thoughts and vain,
And, feeding fond desire, needs must he burn
Unto Cleonae his swift steps turn.
Nor to these matters was the Colchian [Medea] blind,
And though as yet his speech to her was kind,
Good heed she took of all his moody ways,
And how he loved her not as in past days;
And how he shrunk from her, yet knew it not,
She noted, and the stammering words and hot,
Wherewith as she grew kinder still he strove
To hide from her the changing of his love.

[Morris, II, 270-1]

Mackail, his first biographer, hinted that *Jason* described Morris's own marriage. He pointed out that

> Shy and reserved in life . . . [yet] having no concealments from the widest circle of all. . . . In the verses that frame the stories of *The Earthly Paradise* there is an autobiography so delicate and so outspoken that it must needs be left to speak for itself. [Mackail, I, 210]

May Morris, though she was only four or five when her father wrote this passage, also recognized the personal nature of *Jason.* She wrote,

> I always felt, that my father's sympathies were with Medea – not Medea the sorceress, but the woman weak in the very

> strength of her love . . . breathing his own spirit into it: he certainly could not have worked it out in any other way. [Morris, II, xvi-xvii]

As a member of the inner circle Rossetti understood the barely disguised but confessional nature of *Jason.* His response was immediate. He painted Janey as la Pia de Tolomei from Dante's *The Divine Comedy*. In the painting he showed her as a lovely but forlorn woman of the Middle Ages. Her husband's love letters lie by her side together with a devotional book; her fingers gently touch her wedding band. Her name signifies fidelity. When the painting was nearly finished, Rossetti held an elaborate party in April 1868 at his house in Cheyne Walk to unveil the portrait.

He explained to his guests that, in Purgatory, Dante encounters la Pia whose husband had sent her away from Siena and condemned her to exile in the marshes of the Maremma. She asks Dante to "Remember me, who am la Pia, Siena made me, Maremma unmade me, as he knows, who plighted me to him in wedlock with this ring." The message that Rossetti chose to convey was metaphorical but direct: Morris who loved Janey once was now the cause of her misery.

Rossetti knew spousal neglect. Lizzie had died several years before from an overdose of laudanum. The coroner classified her death as a misadventure, though she may have committed suicide. Rossetti was out the evening she died and held himself accountable. Just three months after unveiling Janey as la Pia, Rossetti lambasted Warington Taylor, another insensitive husband. Morris had hired Taylor in 1865 as the office manager for the Firm. Well educated, articulate and argumentative, Taylor had disagreed with his father and been dispossessed. He now fought with his wife who threatened to leave. Women, he felt, had no appreciation of men. Taylor told Philip Webb,

> No man with any genuine enthusiasm in life ought to be otherwise than celibate. Women have no enthusiasm and directly a man is absorbed by his work consider themselves neglected and miserable.

When she finally walked out on him in July 1868, Taylor was devastated. He turned to his friends for help. He asked Webb to ask Morris

("I am ashamed to ask Morris's permission. I am afraid he would think me a fool") to ask Janey to intercede ("She could go and see my wife and tell her what she alone can tell her").

A week or so later Taylor's wife returned and he was ecstatic. He wrote to Webb.

> This is once more the happiness of the past only much greater. What a splendid woman she has been. . . . I left her for some idea which I never attained – gave up a woman of exquisite beauty with a heart full of love to attain some vague notion of a perfection of earnestness . . . There she was all the time working as a servant literally as a servant scrubbing and cleaning for me and all she got in return was an oath total neglect absolute indifference.

He gave a great deal of the credit to Rossetti.

> Gabriel, has told me rightly what I was – he has hit me so hard – How rightly he summed me up. He never was so splendid, so noble, so grand as on Friday when he told me what he thought of it all and what a damned scoundrel I was. [Taylor Papers]

With Morris however Rossetti failed. Morris explained why in verse. In the opening lines of the first volume of *The Earthly Paradise,* a dedicatory poem addressed to Janey, he declared he was incapable of changing himself or helping her. Punning on her maiden name, Burden, he wrote, "I cannot ease the burden of your fears . . . Or bring again the pleasure of past years." As a "dreamer of dreams," he asked, "Why should I strive to set the crooked straight?" [Morris, III, 1].

Biographers have wondered with whom Morris fell in love. Some have suggested Georgie Jones; others have indicated Aglaia Coronio, a beautiful woman of Greek extraction who – like Georgie and Georgie's sister Louisa Baldwin – often provided Morris a sympathetic ear. But Cleonae, who lures Jason from Medea, is a woman whose "loveliness seemed that which he had loved his whole life long" [Morris, II, 270]. In returning to poetry Morris was going back to his inspirational source, his sister. In a sonnet entitled "Near but Far Away" dated "May 11th" that he wrote in 1867 or 1868 (a draft copy of the poem is on paper watermarked 1867, a fair copy on paper marked 1868) he made this clear.

In the poem, the sister turns to look at her brother; her eyes seem damp with tears of renewed regret as she detects the misery he feels but may not articulate. He starts to speak, fighting to overcome restraints of shame, but she stops him. Instead, they kiss as she pulls him into paradise. She then withdraws, leaving him alone with unwelcome truth; pinned down between a threatening sea and a blank wall.

> She wavered, stopped and turned, methought her eyes,
> The deep grey windows of her heart, were wet,
> Methought they softened with a new regret
> To note in mine unspoken miseries,
> And as a prayer from out my heart did rise
> And struggled on my lips in shame's strong net,
> She stayed me, and cried "Brother!" our lips met,
> Her dear hands drew me into Paradise.
> Sweet seemed that kiss till thence her feet were gone,
> Sweet seemed the word she spake, while it might be
> As worldless music – But truth fell on me,
> And kiss and word I knew, and, left alone,
> Face to face seemed I to a wall of stone,
> While at my back there beat a boundless sea.
>
> [May Morris, I, 538-9]

Eight

And think how it be if they were gone not to return

For the first time in his life Morris faced serious money problems. The business of the Firm increased and he earned royalties from the sale of his new books of poetry; however, the income from his inheritance had contracted sharply and he was spending more than he brought in. Warington Taylor estimated in October 1868 that Morris was eating into his capital at the rate of about £200 a year, and worried that his drawing down cash might jeopardize the Firm. He wrote to Webb,

> We have money in hand, and W. M. to satisfy his own conscience would be reckless – he himself having spent just as much over and above his proper income as he did three years ago – ask him what he spent last year – you will be staggered – I know the amount – to ease his conscience he would be reckless in the firm. [Taylor Papers]

The tension at Queen Square consequently intensified. Rossetti wrote to his friend Alice Boyd in November 1868,

> I called on Topsy, who was howling and threatening to throw a new piano of his wife's out of window. It unfortunately arrived I believe just at dinner time and the occurrence had poisoned his peace of mind ever since.

A week later he wrote with even greater sarcasm:

> I met Topsy the other night at a large party of Greeks. He seemed depressed and complained of deafness, but on a large plug of string being taken out of his ear, he revived a good deal and even scratched himself in places apparently inaccessible. When I left, he was being prepared for departure. The whisky cork had already been got out of his nose, and Janey had nearly succeeded in fishing the paper-knife up from the base of his spine. He was offering to stand on his head that it might drop out, but this was thought unnecessary. [Rossetti Letters, II, 673, 675]

Morris resented Rossetti's unsolicited intrusions, but perceived an inviting yet improbable solution. Rossetti would fall in love with Janey and take her off his hands. Rossetti sensed the same improbability. He began to write poetry again, which he had given up since Lizzie's death. The springs of affection, frozen for six years, began to thaw as he opened his heart and soul to the suffering wife of his friend. Having seen her as la Pia, he now envisaged her as Persephone whose gruesome husband bound her to darkness and, more prophetically, as Pandora who opened the magical box from which all the ills of the world flew out but closed it again before Hope escaped.

In a poem written in 1868 or 1869 Morris again described his desire for Emma. He referred to their meeting, as they often did on family holidays, in a conventional fashion, in a normal setting, with their lips sealed against talking of "things I never can forget." He also brought Rossetti and Janey into the poem as well. He imagined the tedious hours before Rossetti would climb the stairs to his living quarters above the workshop at Queen Square and there carry on a casual but false conversation, pretending nothing was amiss between them. Then he imagined how both Janey and Rossetti were gone. Left alone, he dreams of some improbable moment in time when everything has gone up in flames, allowing Emma and him to gain "the boon we talked of as so vain."

> We meet we laugh and talk but still is set
> A seal oer things I never can forget
>
> But must not speak of still I count the hours
> That bring my friend to me with hungry eyes

I watch him as his feet the staircase mount
Then face to face we sit a wall of lies
Made hard by fear and faint anxieties
Is drawn between us and he goes away
And leaves me wishing it were yesterday

Then when they both are gone I sit alone
And turning foolish sleepless pages oer
And think how it be if they were gone
Not to return or worse if the time bore
Some seed of hatred in its fiery core
And nought of praise were left to me to gain
But the boon we talked of as so vain

[Morris MS].

The moment for immolation came early in 1869 when Morris and Burne-Jones decided to leave their wives. Burne-Jones had begun an affair with a beautiful young woman named Mary Zambaco. Unable to have him to herself, she tried to get him to commit suicide. Rossetti wrote to Brown on 23 January 1869,

> She provided herself with laudanum for two at least, and insisted on their winding up matters in Lord Holland's Lane. Ned didn't see it, when she tried to drown herself in the water in front of Browning's house &c. – bobbies collaring Ned who was rolling with her on the stones to prevent it, and God knows what else. [Rossetti Letters, II, 685]

Faced with marital disasters, Morris and Burne-Jones headed for Rome. Uncertain, but expectant Rossetti waited. In a poem written the very next day, the 24 January 1869, he imagined himself as a patient hunter:

Mark me, how still I am! But should there dart
    One moment through thy soul the soft surprise
    Of that winged Peace which lulls the breath of sighs, –
Then shalt thou see me smile, and turn apart
Thy visage to mine ambush at thy heart
    Sleepless with cold commemorative eyes.

[Rossetti Poems, 323-4]

The delinquent husbands got no farther than Dover. Burne-Jones was too ill and distraught to go on. He and Morris returned to London a few days later. Neither had the stomach for total ruin.

It was only six weeks after these tumultuous events that Henry James visited Queen Square. Impressed with Morris, he was absolutely stunned by Janey. He wrote to his sister Alice,

> Ah, *ma chere*, such a wife! *Je n'en reviens pas* – she haunts me still. Imagine, a tall lean woman in a long dress of some dead purple stuff, guiltless of hoops (or of anything else, I should say) with a mass of crisp black hair heaped into great wavy projections on each of her temples, a thin pale face, a pair of strange sad, deep, dark Swinburnish eyes, with great thick black oblique brows, joined in the middle and tucking themselves away under her hair, a mouth like the "Oriana" in our illustrated Tennyson, a long neck, without any collar, and in lieu thereof some dozen strings of outlandish beads – in fine Complete.

After dinner Morris read one of his new poems while Janey lay on a sofa in a corner holding a handkerchief to her face. James saw her as "this dark silent medieval woman" suffering, as he thought, from a painful "medieval toothache" [James Letters, I, 93-4]. Not yet the master of the psychoanalytic, Henry James mistook a broken heart for a bad tooth.

In April, a few weeks after James's visit, Morris began the story of "The Lovers of Gudrun." Begun at Queen Square, the poem was completed in Cheyne Walk where Morris and Janey stayed for several days while Rossetti worked on a new painting of her as Pandora.

Based on Icelandic legend, the story described the mounting tension among the three friends. Kiartan (Morris) feels the irresistible pull of adventure and leaves Gudrun (Janey Morris) to search for fame and honor. She is bereft. She can't understand why he wants to go abroad. She thinks that those who have known real love are content to stay at home. She longs for his return. Eventually, his co-adventurer Bodli (Rossetti) comes bearing the awful news that a foreign king's sister has fallen in love with Kiartan and has kept him from coming home. Distraught, Gudrun turns to Bodli for comfort:

As a grey dove, within the meshes caught,
Flutters a little, then lies still again
Ere wildly beats its wings with its last pain,
So once or twice her passion, as she spake,
Rose to her throat, and yet might not outbreak
Till that last word was spoken; then as stung
By pain on pain, her arms abroad she flung,
And wailed aloud; but the dry-eyed Bodli stood
Pale as a corpse, and in such haggard mood,
Such helpless, hopeless misery, as one
Who first in hell meets her he hath undone
Yet sank her wailing in a little while
Through dreadful sobs to silence, and a smile,
A feeble memory of the courteous ways,
For which in days agone she won such praise,
Rose to her pale lips, and she spake once more
As if the passionate words, cast forth before,
Were clean forgotten, with that bitter wail:

"O, Bodli Thorleikson, of good avail
Thou art to me, and now has come
Swiftly indeed unto a troubled home:
For ill at ease I am, and fain would hear
From thee who know'st him, why this looked-for year
Lacks Kiartan still."

Kiartan eventually returns with glory won. Expecting a joyous welcome, he finds that Gudrun and Bodli have fallen in love:

. . . O Gudrun, Gudrun,
Here I come back with all the honour won
We talked of, that thou saidest thou knewst well
Was but for thee – to whom then shall I tell
The tale of that well-doing?

He accepts the change without quarrel, but is extremely angry:

"Good luck go with them! mine she cannot be,
May she be happy, here, or over sea!
Why should I wish aught ill on them to fall?"

And yet indeed, a flood of bitterest gall
Swept o'er his heart; despite himself he thought:
"So now, to lonely ways behold me brought,
She will not miss me more – so change the days,
And Bodli's loving looks and Bodli's praise
Shall be enough for her. I am alone,
And ne'er shall be aught else – would I were gone
From where none need me now –"
[Morris, V, 310-11, 320, 338]

Not surprisingly, Janey Morris grew sicker as the collapse of her marriage manifested itself in art and poetry. By the summer her condition was so bad that their friends prevailed on Morris to take her on a holiday abroad. Rossetti, Webb, the Joneses and their other friends hoped that a break from work and a return to the continent where they had enjoyed their honeymoon together would restore their marriage.

They arrived at a popular resort town to take the curative waters, but had left without making reservations. As a result "they were literally stranded at the station at Ems," May Morris wrote years later, "and I scarcely know which to be sorrier for, mother waiting there alone in a state of collapse, or father, frantically seeking for accommodation and coming back to her in a positively desperate state of mind" [Morris, V, xii]. Janey was too fragile at first to do much of anything. The "carriage business," Morris wrote to Webb, "shakes her too much" so they did no sightseeing together. Once or twice he "paddled her about the river in a machine like a butter-boat with a knife and fork for oars" [Morris Letters, I, 79]. Otherwise he took long walks by himself and wrote more tales for his next volume while she bathed and rested. Rossetti sent a cute, acute cartoon to Janey showing her drinking a glass of spa water as an antidote for each book of *The Earthly Paradise*. They remained abroad for nearly two months, but Morris would neither put his poetry aside nor try to set the crooked straight.

Amazed at his disaffection and obstinacy Rossetti thought that his friend must soon come to his senses. "The more he loves you," he wrote to Janey, "the more he knows that you are too lovely and noble not to be loved" [DGR-JM Letters, 11]. Noting, in one letter to Philip Webb, the irony of their staying at Bad Ems (Bad as estranged, Ems as Morrises),

Morris implied in another that they were not making love. He wrote in a passage that May Morris expunged when she printed some of her father's letters,

> I turn in at ½ past 10, which is about the time Janey composes herself to sleep: in revenge we get (I get) up early; this morning I was a long way on my road before 9 o'clock.

In a postscript to the same letter Janey concurred. She felt better but saw that Morris had no desire to fix their marriage. She told Webb,

> My finger-tips, are sound as you see by this – and fit for much more hard labour – I feel that I have not much else about me that is good for anything [referring to her husband], but I have a sort of presentiment (though of course you don't believe in such things) that I may make a rapid turn – and feel myself well all of a sudden – and then I have another presentiment that should this change come – all those I now call my Friends would also change – and would not be able to stand me. [Morris Letters, I, 89]

To Webb, and to Morris if he saw what she said, her allusive language was easy to decipher. If her husband could not bring himself to love her again and thereby cure her illness, she would turn for love and health to the man who found her "too lovely and noble not to be loved" even at the risk of losing all of her other friends.

Nine

They have hopes that they are not conscious of

The voyage to Ems brought no reconciliation. While Rossetti remained in limbo, caught in the contradictory roles of family counselor and lover-in-the-wings, Janey patiently waited, drinking and bathing in the waters that were of course no cure for her sickness. After two months abroad, she finally realized that her husband preferred re-discovering love in the dreamland of poetry to loving her. By the end of August she was ready to come home. Husband and wife returned to London with nothing changed, but each with a view to giving new shape to the future.

Morris came to grips with the chronic matter of money. Taylor was particularly concerned that Morris's habit of writing checks for himself against the Firm's account whenever he was short of funds would wreck the business. He wrote to Webb on 12 July 1869, a few days before the Morrises left for Ems,

> I think a stern warning from you, that the firm must be respected when the last £200 is devoured, that its property is sacred, would have some effect upon WM. It will make him think about what is to be done. The sooner he devours his £200 the better – things must then come to a crisis – the firm has served him well – his capital has all along returned him 5 and 6 per cent and is now paid back to him – and he has a nice steady little business – to knock it down would be the utmost folly. [Taylor Papers]

Taylor, like the partners of the firm, was fully aware of Morris's marital problems and more informed than the rest about his finances. He wrote to Webb again in August,

> About WM's own private money affairs, I am very anxious. I think he has a most trying time coming – his only chance is regularly paying his weekly bills now that the mines pay badly as well as irregularly. It is for him a bad situation. The books bring in money at uncertain times – it comes like a 'tip' to a school boy – and is of no real benefit – I only trust he wont come to grief under his trial – since I have been ill during the last 18 months an unsteadiness has grown up – bad – and this causes me anxiety. [Taylor Papers]

Morris acknowledged his financial difficulties to Webb while asking him to advance him sixty pounds against the prospect of running out of funds in Germany. He wanted Webb to know that he was not upset over Taylor's constant reminders. He wrote in a letter on 20 August,

> I hope, he don't think I am seriously vexed at any thing he has said, or otherwise than very much obliged by his friendliness; I think I understand the whole matter perfectly well; and know there is a great deal of reason in what he says, though he is not at present quite master of the details. [Morris Letters, I, 92]

Toward the end of their stay in Ems, Rossetti suggested that Morris should take Janey to Switzerland, but as Morris pointed out to Webb, there were a number of reasons, including the lack of money, why they should return home instead.

Sometime during the last six months of his life, Taylor helped Morris pull together a responsible budget. In 1868 he had estimated that Morris was spending from £1,000 to £1,100 a year, an amount that was rapidly depleting his resources. Taylor figured that Morris received about £460 from dividends from the shares that he had inherited from his father in the Devon Great Consolidated Copper Mining Company, down by half from the £900 per year he received when he came of age in 1855. In 1874 the copper company ceased paying dividends altogether.

Taylor calculated that Morris also obtained about £200 a year from the sale of his books and another £200 from his salary as manager of the Firm. The roughly £200 shortfall – the difference between his spending (£1060) and his income (£860) – came from drawing down cash that Morris had invested in the Firm. In October 1868, Morris had £400 left to claim; by August 1869 the amount was down to £200.

Morris took the problem seriously. He began making lists of annual expenditures that totaled half of what he had spent in 1868. In March 1870, the month after Taylor died, he persuaded the other members of the Firm to increase his salary by fifty pounds, assume the cost of the rent, taxes, gas and coal at Queen Square and give him a ten per cent share of the Firm's net income. In 1871 he added another £100 to his income by becoming a director of the rapidly declining copper mining company.

While Morris and Janey were abroad, Rossetti asked and received official permission to open Lizzie's grave to obtain the manuscript poems that, in a state of grief, he had placed in her casket. He especially wanted to retrieve his long poem called "Jenny." He intended to merge the early poems with the poems that he had written during the past twelve months inspired by Janey. Aside from the similarity in names, the Janey poems and "Jenny" expressed Rossetti's deep sympathy for the vulnerable woman under duress. His book of poetry, entitled *Poems,* appeared in April 1870. Morris joined Swinburne and others in writing favorable reviews for the major periodicals.

Privately, to his new admirer Aglaia Coronio, Morris expressed his distaste: "I have done my review, just this moment – ugh!" [Morris Letters, I, 116].

Janey, after returning to England, finally accepted her husband's estrangement and she now began for the first time to see Rossetti alone. Their visits were not joyous nor particularly secretive but cloaked in sadness. Rossetti wrote to her in a note in January 1870,

> The sight of you going down the dark steps to the cab all alone, has plagued me ever since – I hope you got home safe and well. Now everything will be dark for me till I can see you again.[DGR-JM Letters, 33].

In early April, before *Poems* appeared, Janey accepted an invitation to stay at Scalands, the home of Barbara Bodichon, in Sussex. Mrs.

Bodichon, who was a founder of Girton College, Cambridge and a leading advocate of women's rights, also invited Rossetti. Janey and Rossetti were together at Scalands for much of April and May.

On April 26 Morris wrote Janey a seemingly cordial note:

> I scarcely dared hope you would get so much better. On Sunday I did a good days work at the Venusberg and sat up till 3 ½ last night writing it all out; I think I may finish this last part this week, but then I have to rewrite a good deal of the earlier part. [Morris Letters, I, 117]

The Venusberg referred to "The Hill of Venus," the last tale that Morris wrote for the final volume of *The Earthly Paradise*. It is unlikely that Janey missed the layers of irony in her husband's communication. Writing on the day of their wedding anniversary, he is delighted that she suddenly feels well, out of his sight and in the company of Rossetti, allowing him, undisturbed at home, to stay up all night to complete his imaginary exploration of the mound of Venus. In the tale, Walter, a German knight despairing of life, finds refuge in a dark, overgrown cavern in the hillside. Within, he discovers Venus, beautiful, naked and direct. She approaches with hands held out, "her blood throbbing as his throbbed through her bosom sweet" [Morris, VI, 294].

Sometime between 1869 and 1871, Morris started a novel in a contemporary setting that he eventually abandoned. (The manuscript is written throughout on paper watermarked 1869, but Mackail indicates that it was written in 1871.) In the story he tackled the problem that now nagged him deeply. The major character, Parson Risley, has grown angry and unhappy because he has married a woman other than the one he loved. Morris gives the story a dramatic turn when he has the wife discover a letter that her husband wrote to his true love years before.

In the letter, the Parson describes how he came up to London to confess that he was going to marry another woman, but lost his nerve. In an extraordinary gush of words he reveals that his resolve was overpowered by infatuation. He tells his sweetheart that

> when you took me upstairs to see your newly furnished bedroom, and were so pretty over talking about all the things, and showed me your dear clothes in the drawers and I saw your

> little slippers lying about, and all the dear things that touch your body that I love so, then my heart failed me as I thought I should never be with you in the new pretty bed, and I came away with the kisses that I feel now.

He simply couldn't tell her in person that he was to be married next Thursday. Confused and distraught he says the most preposterous things. "Who knows," he continues in the letter, "– we may meet again – my wife may die before we are either of us very old." He asks for pity, forgiveness, understanding, love and reunion:

> You know dear that life won't be very pleasant to me, so don't be too angry: at all events be sure that I don't love her: ugh!. . . oh my God if I were only back with you to give and be forgiven over and over again how can I do it how can I do it? To live and pretend to love this ugly stupid woman, bad-hearted too she is – when I have had the cleverest and most beautiful woman in the world in my arms. [Morris Papers]

Morris sent the manuscript of this nascent novel to Georgie Burne-Jones to see if she would give him any encouragement. She gave him none.

Janey Morris understood how her husband felt towards her. Did she also know his feelings for his sister? In the last months of 1870, while Morris finished the final revisions to the fourth and last volume of *The Earthly Paradise*, Janey stayed several weeks with Morris's mother and his sisters Henrietta and Emma in Torquay. On 25 November, Morris wrote to her to say that the last volume would be published in time for the holidays. He asked her to tell his sister that he would have a nice surprise for her. The sentence is incomplete but revealing:

> Tell Emmie I shall have a Christmas present for her which I hope may tend in some degree toward counteracting a youth spent in – ah! – Have the kids written? [Morris Letters, I, 126-7]

What might he have added to finish the sentence? A youth spent in "reading stirring romances together," or "daydreaming about love and heavenly reunion?" We can only guess, but we can be sure that Janey understood the allusion and its irony. A Christmas gift to his sister of the final volume of *The Earthly Paradise*, with its concluding tale of "The Hill of Venus," would serve not to "counteract" but rather celebrate and, in a sense, consummate his love.

A week or so later, in another letter to Janey, Morris interrupted himself again. In response to her writing about the pain of unhappiness he countered that sensitive and imaginative people always have hope:

> As for living, dear, people like you speak about dont know either what life or death means, except for one or two supreme moments of their lives, when something pierces through the crust of dullness and ignorance, and they act for the time as if they were sensitive people –
>
> For me I don't think people really want to die because of mental pain, that is if they are imaginative people; they want to live to see the play played out fairly – they have hopes that they are not conscious of –
>
> Hillao! here's cheerful talk for you – I beg your pardon, dear, with all my heart [Morris Letters, I, 128].

Morris didn't need to complete the thought. Janey knew what hopes he harbored.

Chapter Ten

As my twin sister, young of years was she and slender

With the appearance of the final volume of *The Earthly Paradise* in December 1870, Morris found himself "in the condition of mind that comes over people who are taking leave of a big piece of work" [Morris, VI, x]. The five books (if we include *Jason* which he planned as the first of the many stories comprising the entire series) occupied him for nearly five years and coincided with, and to some extent documented, the disintegration of his marriage. He wrote to Janey in November 1870,

> I feel rather lost at having done my book, I find now I liked working at it better than I thought – I must try and get something serious to do as soon as may be. [Morris Letters, I, 126]

He now turned his attention to Iceland. Two years earlier he met Eirikr Magnussson under whose guidance he began to study Icelandic literature, which found expression in his story "The Lovers of Gudrun." With Magnusson and Charles Faulkner, he planned a journey to Iceland for the summer of 1871. At the same time he began casting about for a summer retreat for Janey and his daughters. In the early spring he saw an advertisement for a house in the country not far from Oxford and went to investigate. He liked what he saw. To Faulkner on 17 May 1871 he wrote:

> I have been looking about for a house for the wife and kids, and whither do you guess my eye is turned now? Kelmscott, a little village about two miles above Radcott Bridge – a heaven on earth; an old stone Elizabethan house like Water Eaton, and such a garden! close down on the river, a boat house and all things handy. I am going there again on Saturday with Rossetti and my wife: Rossetti because he thinks of sharing it with us if the thing looks likely. [Morris Letters, I, 133]

Morris and Rossetti signed the lease of Kelmscott Manor soon after the visit and became tenants in common.

Six weeks later Janey, Jenny and May were lodged at Kelmscott, and Morris was on his way to Iceland. He worried whether they would have sufficient food, but Janey reassured him that they were properly provisioned. He wrote from Queen Square on 6 July, the eve of his departure,

> I am delighted that Victuals won't fail you, truth to say I was a little nervous on this point – How beautiful the place looked last Monday: I grudged going away so; but I am very happy to think of you all happy there, and the children & you getting wel." [Morris Letters, I, 139]

For Morris the voyage to Iceland had special significance. It was a physical adventure to a remote and primitive land and a chance for Rossetti and Janey to live together in a quiet and out-of-the-way place. Aboard the fortnightly mailboat from Edinburgh to Reykjavik, he was at first nervous about the undertaking, and recorded in the opening pages of his diary,

> That morning, my heart failed me and I felt as if I should have been glad of any accident that had kept me at home; yet now it would have seemed unbearable to sleep in London another night. [Morris, VIII, 1]

From Reykjavik he and his companions endured an exhausting journey over the volcanic terrain to the valley of the Markfleet, reaching the ridge overlooking the great glacier on 22 July. Morris experienced a sense of awe, triumph and release:

> I could see its whole dismal length now, crowned with overhanging glaciers from which the water dripped in numberless falls that seemed to go nowhere . . . at right angles to this mountain was the still higher wall that closed the valley, . . . below was the flat black plain space of the valley, and all about it every kind of distortion and disruption, and the labyrinth of the furious brimstone-laden Markfleet winding amidst it lay between us and anything like smoothness: surely it was what I 'came out for to see,' yet for the moment I felt cowed, and as if I should never get back again: yet with that came a feeling of exultation too, and I seemed to understand how people under all disadvantages should find their imaginations kindle amid such scenes. [Morris, VIII, 54]

The exhilarating trip lasted nearly two months. When he reached the post office at Reykjavik on 24 August, he experienced a letdown. He read his letters from London "with not more than the usual amount of disappointment, wondering at people's calmness" [Morris, VIII, 178]. Did he hope to hear from someone that his marriage was over?

The calm was ruffled a few weeks after his return to England. For the October issue of the *Contemporary Review*, Robert Buchanan wrote a scathing article entitled "The Fleshly School of Poetry: D.G. Rossetti." A Scots poet and minor literary figure in London, Buchanan charged that Rossetti's conception of love was fleshly rather than ideal. He insinuated that his poetic and artistic inspiration came from illicit experiences. He cited as an example the poem of "Jenny" which conveyed understanding and sympathy for a young prostitute. Although disturbed, Rossetti shrugged off the attack.

At the same time Morris was pleased to show Rossetti the preliminary draft of his new work. Rossetti liked what he read, telling William Bell Scott,

> The poem is, I think, at a higher point of execution perhaps than anything he has done, having a passionate lyric quality such as one found in his earliest work, and of course much more mature balance in carrying it out. It will be a very fine work. [Mackail, I, 280]

The complete title of the new work was *Love is Enough; or, The Freeing of Pharamond: A Morality*. So that his readers would grasp the thrust of the book-length poem, Morris presented an "Argument" at the beginning. It said,

> This story, which is told by way of a morality set before an Emperor and Empress newly wedded, showeth of a king whom nothing but love might satisfy, who left all to seek love, and having found it, found this also, that he had enough, though he lacked all else.

As he did so often in his imaginative writing, Morris spoke his mind. The recently married emperor and empress are projections of Rossetti and Janey. Morris is king Pharamond, who through the medium of the morality, sets out to explain himself. The king abdicates his responsibilities, freeing himself to find his love. His subjects are mystified by his action; one Northern Lord rebukes him sharply for succumbing to calf-love:

> Are they lies, these fair tidings, or what see thy lords here –
> Some love-sick girl's brother caught up by that sickness,
> As one street beggar catches the pest from his neighbor?

Undeterred, Pharamond leaves everyone behind to seek love, whom he calls Azalais. He eventually finds her in a woodland garden, in the shape of his sister:

> Through the boughs of the garden I followed the singing
> To a smooth space of sward: there the unknown desire
> Of my soul I beheld, – wrought in the shape of a woman....
> As my twin sister, young of years was she and slender,
> Yellow blossoms of spring-tide her hands had been gathering,
> But the gown-lap that held them had fallen adown
> And had lain round her feet with the first of the singing.

Pharamond's vision is hazy and romantic, but his moral is clear: it is better to be free in the quest of love than to remain mired in the mundane. Pure love, in short, is sufficient. Even so, Pharamond makes an important concession: "—Yea, Love were enough if thy lips were not lacking" [Morris, IX, 19, 29, 75]. The book was finished in the autumn of 1872 and published in November. Morris sent a copy to his sister inscribed "Emma Oldham from her most affectionate Brother William Morris. Dec. 7th 1872" [Morris Collection].

In May 1872 Buchanan renewed his attack on Rossetti by expanding and reissuing his article as a pamphlet. Two weeks later, Robert Browning sent Rossetti a gift copy of his new poem. Reading *Fifine at the Fair,* Rossetti became convinced that Browning and Buchanan were conspiring against him. He read how Don Juan deserts his "spiritual lady" (Lizzie) for the earthly delights of the gipsy Fifine (Janey). He was furious. He could endure the attack of a non-entity like Buchanan, but not that of a good friend. Rossetti suffered a serious mental collapse. When she heard the news Janey hastened from Kelmscott to London to be near him in early June. Rossetti's friends felt that it was better to keep them apart, and he soon left for Scotland to recover. He spent nearly three months there before, at the end of September, he felt well enough to return to Kelmscott.

Janey spent most of the summer at Kelmscott with her children. Morris visited frequently and guests arrived from time to time. Around the end of August Philip Webb paid a visit, and he witnessed some untoward event that "gave my soul a twist wh I hope my face did not express, as it was quite unavoidable (in the unfortunate circumstances)." We cannot know exactly what Webb saw or heard, but we can surmise that Morris exploded at Janey. Morris could no longer endure the fact that Rossetti and Janey had not declared themselves *de facto* partners. He wanted his freedom.

Janey wrote to Webb afterwards. Referring to the unfortunate circumstances, she apologized for what he had witnessed. Webb expressed his sympathy in a reply dated 7 September 1872. Perhaps recalling the postscript that she had written from Ems three years before about her presentiment of losing all of her friends, he told her,

> Of course I know the strength of resource in despair, well enough – that is, the willingly cutting one self off from the help of any one, so as to avoid the risk of being deserted by them – but, "nothing venture . . ." you know – well, one

> must venture in friends help, for such a thing to be possible; and assured friendship is very beautiful, and at times deeply soothing in the mere belief in it.

Janey thanked him for his reassurance, but wanted to make sure that he knew that she was telling the truth. Morris was still her husband, though he had lost interest in her and was willing to countenance Rossetti as her lover. The circumstances were not what she wanted, but she was playing the hand she was given.

Webb wrote again to say that he never doubted her honesty and indeed admired the way she handled her difficulties. He told her,

> There is something in human nature pure and simple, wh touches me dearly, and when I see any one clinging to the natural parts of life, I feel much inclined to become one of their friends . . . I have always taken a great interest in you, and none the less that time has tossed all of us about, and made us play other parts than we set out upon – I see that you play yours well and truly under the changes, and I feel deeply sympathetic on that account – for my own troubles are not so absorbing that I cannot attend to the troubles of those who are wrapt about with the pains of life wh are not ignoble. Please believe that I in no way wish to penetrate into sorrows wh I can in no way relieve; I, from my own self, know the impossibility of two people bearing one's burden [a pun on Janey's maiden name]. [Morris Papers]

Webb admired Janey for the dignity with which she bore the pain of rejection and the unpretending way that she found such solace as she could from her friendship with Rossetti.

Eleven

How can I help it, not knowing whether I am on my head or my heels

Morris felt trapped. Janey would not leave him to live with Rossetti (though she would allow Rossetti to live with her at Kelmscott). Morris had neither the disposition nor the justification to forcibly end their marriage. Hoisted like an errant knight on his own petard, Morris was stuck. He turned to Aglaia Coronio for sympathy.

She was married to Theodore Coronio, a member of the wealthy and well-connected community of Greek ex-patriots living in London. Her father was Luke Ionides, who had fled from Constantinople in the 1820s before the advance of Turkish forces. She was the same age as Morris and, like him, had two children. Much admired for her beauty and good sense she liked the arts and befriended artists. She met Morris sometime in the late 1860s, but their friendship began around 1870 and blossomed. Morris relished her attention and found her a sympathetic listener. He modified her name (Aglaia) for the name of Pharamond's love in *Love is Enough* (Azalais).

At the end of September 1872 Rossetti recovered sufficiently to leave Scotland and return to Kelmscott. His re-appearance impinged on Morris. On October 8, he wrote to Aglaia,

> I have been backwards and forwards to Kelmscott a good deal this summer and autumn; but shall not go there so often now as Gabriel is come there, and talks of staying there permanently: of course he won't do that, but I suppose he

> will stay some time: he is quite well and seems very happy. [In contrast Morris had been feeling ill. He continued] The weather, has been lovely here this autumn, but doesn't seem to have suited me very well, I have been queer several times, and am not very brilliant today – As to my mental health – I have had ups and downs as you may very easily imagine. [Morris Letters, I, 165]

Morris confided his queerness to Aglaia. He admitted to her that he was unsure why he felt so down since no one harangued him for allowing his marriage to fall apart. He wrote on 25 November,

> When I said, there was no cause for my feeling low, I meant that my friends had not changed at all towards me in any way and that there had been no quarrelling: and indeed I am afraid it comes from some cowardice or unmanliness in me.

He was also no longer certain what he believed. Attenuating what he had said in *Love is Enough* (which appeared the week that he wrote this letter) about the singular importance of true love, he told her,

> One thing wanting ought not to go for so much: nor indeed does it spoil my enjoyment of life always, as I have often told you: to have real friends and some sort of an aim in life is so much, that I ought still to think myself lucky: and often in my better moods I wonder what it is in me that throws me into such rage and despair at other times: I suspect, do you know, that some such moods would have come upon me at times even without this failure of mine. [Morris Letters, I, 172-3]

By now, Morris realized that Rossetti might indeed remain at Kelmscott. The prospect disturbed him immensely. He complained to Aglaia,

> another quite selfish business is that Rossetti has set himself down at Kelmscott as if he never meant to go away; and not only does that keep me away from that harbour of refuge,

> (because it is really a farce our meeting when we can help it) but also he has all sorts of ways so unsympathetic with the sweet simple old place, that I feel his presence there as a kind of a slur on it: this [is] very unreasonable though when one thinks why one took the place, and how this year it has really answered that purpose: nor do I think I should feel this about it if he had not been so unromantically discontented with it & the whole thing which made me very angry and disappointed – There, dear Aglaia see how I am showing you my pettinesses! *please* dont encourage me in them; but you have always been so kind to me that they will come out. O how I long to keep the world from narrowing on me, and to look at things bigly and kindly! [Morris Letters, I, 172-3].

Morris closed the letter by telling her that he planned another trip to Iceland as the previous trip had done him such good: "I am going to try to go to Iceland next year, hard as it will be to drag myself away from two or three people in England: but I know there will be a kind of rest in it, let alone the help it will bring me from physical reasons: I know clearer now perhaps than then what a blessing & help last years journey was to me; or what horrors it saved me from" [Morris Letters, I, 172-3].

Towards the end of the year Morris found a new house in town for his family. The growth of the Firm required a move as the residence on the upper floors at Queen Square were needed for expansion. He told Aglaia, "Janeys room has already got the workmans benches in it: the big room is bare and painty: there is hammering and sawing & running up and down stairs going on." He leased what he described as "a *very* little house with a pretty garden: and I think will suit Janey & the children." His daughter Jenny had just turned twelve, and though the fact made him feel older, the move had made him feel better. He wrote in February,

> We are quite settled in our new house, and I find it very pleasant: my own room is particularly cheerful & pretty, and I can work in it with a much better heart than in the dingy room at Queen Sq [Morris Letters, I, 177-9].

Located in Turnham Green in Hammersmith, the house provided him a healthy walk to and from the Firm.

In April Morris went with Burne-Jones to Italy. For Burne-Jones the trip was an important artistic event, but for Morris it gave little satisfaction. He got more enjoyment from seeing the countryside than viewing the arts and spent more time than Burne-Jones approved of shopping for inventory. He wrote to Janey,

> It was something also to remember, coming down into the plain of Piedmont out of the Alps; on the most beautiful of all evenings, and going (still between snow-capped mountains) through a country like a garden: green grass & feathery poplars, and abundance of pink blossomed leafless peach & almond trees.

In Florence he bought "a lot of queer pots" used for hand warmers and wickered flasks in a variety of pretty shapes to ship back to the Firm. He pronounced the Duomo the most beautiful church in the world outside" but found the inside "as bare as the palm of my hand" [Morris Letters, I, 183]. The restoration of San Miniato appalled him, and he saw little of interest in Siena. He wrote to Webb,

> I am not at all disappointed with Italy; but a good deal with myself; I am happy enough, but as a pig is, and cannot bring my mind up to the proper pitch and tune for taking in these marvels. [Morris Letters, I, 185]

He decided to cut the trip short, leaving Burne-Jones to travel alone.

Morris prepared for his second journey to Iceland with decidedly mixed feelings. He felt the return to the cold and savage island as needful therapy, but like a patient resisted a sometimes painful treatment. He sailed with Faulkner again (but not Magnusson) aboard the same ship (Diana) occupying the same berth as two years before. He wrote to Webb,

> Lord how strange I felt, to be in the little cabin again! I feel grave enough & not much as if this were a pleasant trip, but hope to get something out of it all; and (though

> you may think that unreasonable) to come back again at last" [Morris Letters, I, 195]

A week later he wrote to Janey, saying that he had arrived safely at Reykjavik. "It is all like a kind of a dream to me," he confessed, "and my real life seems set aside till it is over." He ended the letter with a conciliatory note:

> My dear how I wish I was back, & how wild & strange everything here is. I am so anxious for you too. It was a grievous parting for us the other day. And this shabby letter! but how can I help it, not knowing whether I am on my head or my heels. [Morris Letters, I, 196]

He told Aglaia when he returned two months later that the voyage had on him its hoped-for effect:

> the glorious simplicity of the terrible & tragic, but beautiful land with its well remembered stories of brave men, killed all querulous feeling in me, and have made all the dear faces of wife & children, and love, & friends dearer than ever to me: I hope I shall not miss your face from among them for long. [Morris Letters, I, 198]

On his return from Iceland Morris began to think of re-organizing the Firm. During the previous twelve years the company had grown in size and reputation. Morris had run the business with some success, despite his personal ups and downs. Rossetti had been instrumental in gaining the company its first notable commission at St. James's Palace, and the artistic work of Rossetti, Burne-Jones, Brown, Webb as well as Morris had attracted an increasingly wide and wealthy clientele. Morris worked hard, if intermittently, and wrung a tolerable livelihood from his efforts. But he knew that the Firm could achieve more. "I should very much like to make the business quite a success," he had written to Aglaia in February, "and it can't be unless I work at it myself" [Morris Letters, I, 178]. He set about to make a change. His decision was hastened by the total cessation of dividends from the Devon Great Consolidated Copper Mining Company.

Sometime around the end of 1873 Morris made it clear to his six partners that he wanted to assume sole control. Brown objected. He thought it unfair that Morris should ask the others to cede their interest just as the Firm was beginning to prosper. He, Marshall and Rossetti turned to Theodore Watts for legal counsel in January 1874. Watts (later Watts-Dunton) was a solicitor and occasional literary critic, and from 1879 he shared his house in Putney with Swinburne. Morris reacted angrily to their resistance. In March Rossetti's brother married Brown's daughter. Invited to the wedding, Morris complained bitterly to Louisa Baldwin, Georgie's sister. He wrote to her on 26 March:

> – Sad grumbling – but do you know I have got to go to a wedding next Tuesday: to wit Lucy Brown & William Rossetti, & it enrages me to think that I lack courage to say, "I don't care for either of you & you neither of you care for me, & I wont waste a day out of my precious life in grinning a company grin at you two old boobies" (for they *are* old Louie, I mean for that sort of folly) [he was forty-five and she thirty-one] – No, I am going, woe worth the while! & hence these tears. [Morris Letters, I, 218-9]

Three weeks later Morris got after Rossetti. Annoyed with his occupation of Kelmscott, Morris wrote him a short, sharp note on 16 April:

> I send herewith the £17.10 to you, not knowing where else to send it since Kinch [the leasing agent] is dead. As to the future though I will ask you to look upon me as off my share, & not to look upon me as shabby for that, since you have fairly taken to living at Kelmscott, which I suppose neither of us thought the other would do when we first began the joint possession of the house; for the rest I am both too poor &, by compulsion of poverty, too busy to be able to use it much in any case, and am very glad if you find it useful & pleasant to you. [Morris Letters, I, 222]

Instead of assuming the lease and staying on, Rossetti decided to leave Kelmscott in July and never returned.

Negotiations among the partners went slowly. Morris wanted the others to turn the Firm over to him, as the one who had for thirteen years done the lion's share of the work and assumed the major financial risks. Brown felt Morris had been compensated for his management and his capital and the business belonged to all seven partners equally. He held, moreover, that the Firm's value in the event of dissolution should include a good measure of "goodwill." Rossetti wished to reach an amicable resolution. He wrote a long note to Brown on 21 October. He postulated that neither Morris nor the other partners had achieved their objectives (irrespective of whether they had any clear expectations to begin with); therefore, none of the partners were willing to take the financial risk, which Morris apparently had proposed, of investing to expand the business now. "I have said both to you and to Morris," he wrote, "that I consider his proceeding sudden and arbitrary," but he was sure that there was room for understanding and compromise. He finished by offering to ask Morris to meet the two of them one evening with no one else present [Rossetti Letters, III, 1315].

Brown spurned Rossetti's overture. "As to Morris," he wrote in reply,

> I could never meet him again with the least pleasure – but even if I could, at the present juncture it would disturb all our negotiations, which are going on satisfactorily in Watts's hand – for I only wish to be clear of the whole affair which I now blush at having ever belonged to. I wish to be quit of it as soon as I can without ridicule – for I am not inclined to go at Morris's dictation. [Angeli, 115]

Brown was in no mood for compromise. His son Nolly had fallen ill on 8 October and died on 5 November.

Watts finally effected a settlement in March 1875. Morris, Marshall, Faulkner & Company was formally dissolved. It was agreed that Morris would pay Brown, Marshall and Rossetti £1,000 each. Faulkner, Webb and Burne-Jones relinquished their interests without compensation. Rossetti made provision that his money would be turned over to Janey. On 31 March, Morris issued a circular announcing that the old firm had been dissolved and would resume under the sole management and ownership of William Morris, as Morris & Co. The circular also stated that Webb and Burne-Jones would continue to provide designs for stained glass and furnishings.

Chapter Twelve

The world goes on, beautiful and strange and dreadful and worshipful

"I have got my partnership business settled at last," Morris declared on 27 May 1875, "and am sole lord & master here now" [Morris Letters, I, 254]. The same day he returned from his last meeting as a director of the copper mining company. Having received his director's fee of £100, he resigned, went home and sat down on his top hat, the sartorial symbol of his corporate authority.

For some time he had wanted to make fabrics that satisfied his eye for design and color. He heartily disliked the bright hues that new advances in chemical engineering had made available. He preferred the muted colors of traditional dyes made from natural sources. He sensed, correctly, that there was a market for beautiful work that transcended the commonplace. In July 1875 he made the first of several trips to Leek in Staffordshire to work first-hand with Thomas Wardle, a master dyer, in order to produce the fine fabric that he had in mind. The work was at once exhilarating and frustrating. He wrote to Aglaia from Queen Square in October,

> We have got a few pieces of printed cloths here, and they are hung up in the big room, where they look so beautiful (really) that I feel inclined to sit and stare at them all day. [Morris Letters, I, 271]

Morris fretted however that Wardle was unable to get the colors he wanted with any consistency. One of the culprits was a dyer named

Kay. He "does not seem to be able to do anything, even the simplest matching, and it is all a matter of luck how things go." Morris thought no better of the other workers, calling them "monsters of idiocy." He wanted absolute success. He tried to make himself perfectly clear to Wardle, warning him that,

> I am prepared to give up all that part of my business which depends on textiles if I fail in getting [the results I want, but insisting], I don't in the least see why I should talk about failing which is after all impossible. [Morris Letters, I, 272, 275, 282]

The results came slowly at first. To speed matters Morris began setting up his own dying vats and looms at Queen Square. He researched old texts for forgotten methods, experimented widely and designed a variety of new patterns for rugs, draperies and tapestries. Morris hired the son of his old tutor Reverend Guy as a secretary and general helper. For several months young Guy recorded the frenetic activity. He wrote on 18 May 1877,

> Mr. Morris slept last night in town, and was up on the move when I arrived. He had been downstairs and set the new dye-pot at work, ready for him to set an indigo vat in the afternoon. . . . G. W. [Morris's manager] and W.M. talked over Mrs. Baring's house in Devonshire: the work we have proposed to do will certainly take two or three years before all completed: we have to get our Lyons silk-weaver at work for one thing.

With Wardle's help, Morris hired a French brocade-weaver named Bazin from Lyons who arrived at the end of June. As Morris had envisaged beautiful fabrics proved irresistible, and his new product lines began to attract wealthy clients. On 8 October he set out with his packages of samples and patterns of "carpets, silks, chintzes, etc." to show the Countess of Charleville in Tullamore, Ireland [Mackail, I, 353-4, 357]. Two years after reorganization, Morris & Co. stood at the edge of prosperity.

For a time the press of business overshadowed poetry in Morris's life. After *Love is Enough*, he worked at translations and worried a little that his creative imagination might be falling off.

He wrote to Aglaia in early 1873,

> My translations go on apace, but I am doing nothing original. It cant be helped though sometimes I begin to fear I am losing my invention. You know I very much wish not to fall off in imagination and enthusiasm as I grow older: there have been men who once upon a time have done things good or noteworthy who have got worse with time and outlived their power: I don't like that at all. [Morris Letters, I, 178]

The brief hiatus in creative poetry ended when Morris gained control of the Firm. In the middle of 1875 he began to write *Sigurd the Volsung*. The book, which he "regarded as his highest achievement in literature" [Mackail, I, 311], expressed his new confidence in himself.

Drawing on the Icelandic saga, Morris narrated the life of the warrior Sigurd from the time of his father through the death of his wife. The heart of the story, which lies in book three and describes Sigurd's love for Brynhild and his marriage to Gudrun, was essentially Morris's story. Sigurd's love for Brynhild is true love at first sight. His marriage to Gudrun is simply fortuitous. Sigurd climbs the mountain Hindfell on his horse Greyfell. There he discovers a body clad in armor lying on the ground. He stops to investigate:

> So thereby he stopeth and kneeleth, for he deems it were good indeed
> If the breath of life abide there and the speech to help at need;
> And as sweet as the summer wind from a garden under the sun
> Cometh forth in the topmost Hindfell the breath of the sleeping-one.
> Then he saith he will look on the face, if it bear him love or hate,
> On the bonds for life's constraining, and the sundering doom of fate.

It is Brynhild and he loves her instantly:

> So he draweth the helm from the head, and, lo, the brow snow-white,
> And the smooth unfurrowed cheeks, and the wise lips breathing light;
> And the face of a woman it is, and the fairest that ever was born,
> Shown forth to the empty heavens and the desert world forlorn:
> But he looketh, and loveth her sore, and he longeth her spirit to move,
> And awaken her heart to the world, that she may behold him and love.
> And he toucheth her breast and her hands, and he loveth her passing sore;
> And he saith: "Awake! I am Sigurd; . . .

Brynhild opens her eyes and experiences instant love as well:

> Then they turned and were knit together; and oft and o'er again
> They craved, and kissed rejoicing, and their hearts were full and fain.

All would be well for Brynhild and Sigurd but fate intervenes. Sigurd drinks a magic potion that makes him forget her and induces him to fall in love with Gudrun.

Gudrun senses that Sigurd's affection lies elsewhere; she knows that he is a better match than she deserves, but she determines to have him and love him anyway:

> As Sigurd's love unhoped-for her barren bosom warms;
> A little while she struggleth with the fear of his mighty fame,
> That grows with her hope's fulfillment; ruth rises with wonder and shame;
> For the kindness grows in her soul, as forgotten anguish dies,

> And her heart feels Sigurd's sorrow in the breast whereon she lies;
> Then the fierce love overwhelms her, and as wax in the fervent fire
> All dies and is forgotten in the sweetness of desire;
> And close she clingeth to Sigurd, as one that hath gotten the best,
> And fair things of the world she deemeth, as a place of infinite rest.

Swearing undying devotion to one another, Sigurd and Gudrun marry. Soon however the potion wears off. Unwilling to hide the truth, Sigurd tells Gudrun that he loves and has always loved Brynhild.

Brynhild in the meantime has married Gunnar. Their marriage also fails, as Gunnar discovers that Brynhild loves Sigurd. Depressed by these revelations Brynhild lapses into a deadly decline. Sigurd tries to rally her. He reminds her of the world of responsibilities. He speaks of "the hope of deeds to do," but the weight of her disappointment is too heavy. In a final effort to save her Sigurd offers to leave Gudrun and take Brynhild away:

> Then once again spake Sigurd, once only and no more:
> A pillar of light all golden he stood on the sunlit floor;
> And his eyes were the eyes of Odin, and his face was the hope of the world,
> And his voice was the thunder of even when the bolt o'er the mountain is hurled:
> The fairest of all things fashioned he stood 'twixt life and death,
> And the Wrath of Regin rattled, and the rings of the Glittering Heath,
> As he cried: "I am Sigurd the Volsung, and belike the tale shall be true
> That no hand on the earth may hinder what my hand would fashion and do:
> And what God or what man shall gainsay it if our love be greater than these,

> The pride and the glory of Sigurd, and the latter days' increase?
> O live, live, Brynhild belov'd! and thee on the earth will I wed,
> And put away Gudrun the Niblung – and all those shall be as dead."

Brynhild is unable to accept either the challenge or the offer. It is too late. [Morris, XII, 123-4, 173-4, 214, 223].

Morris finished writing the third part of *Sigurd* at the end of March 1876 while working at Leek with Wardle. Its conclusion finally brought closure to an important part of his life. From Leek he wrote a long, heartfelt letter to his sister, who was going through difficult times.* He expressed his grief for her state of depression, his desire to do whatever possible to help and his conviction that life is mysterious but compelling. He acknowledged he felt healthy and had lots of interesting work to do, but was willing to sacrifice all for her. "I wish I could say something

* Mackail published the letter in his biography. He did not identify the recipient, but said that Morris wrote it "to a friend who was passing through one of those darknesses in which the whole substance of life seems now and then to crumble away under our hands" [Mackail, I, 327]. The letter has since disappeared.

Philip Henderson believed the letter was written to either Edward or Georgiana Burne-Jones [Henderson, 165]. Fiona MacCarthy favored Edward [MacCarthy, 364]. There is however no evidence that either Burne-Jones was experiencing such difficulties at this time that would occasion such a letter. Norman Kelvin suggested that, "It is equally possible that the recipient was Jane Morris" [Morris Letters, I, 291]. She suffered her most painful moments in the late 1860s. By 1876, when the letter was written, she had recovered a great deal of her equanimity.

I believe that Morris wrote the letter to his sister because she was the woman he loved most deeply. It is likely that during his visits to Leek he saw her frequently, since Leek is about thirty miles from Clay Cross where she lived. It is likely that she was deeply troubled at this time. She had lost two of her three children, her husband's career in the Church had not advanced and her generous giving to local charities diminished her wealth. By 1876 her income from the copper mining company, like her brother's, had ceased. Morris's words of comfort in the letter, moreover, resonate closely with Sigurd's effort to arouse Brynhild at the end of part three of the book. The lines in the letter and the comparable lines in the book were written within weeks, if not days, of each other.

that would serve you," he told her, "beyond what you know very well, that I love you and long to help you: and indeed I entreat you (however trite the words may be) to think that life is not empty nor made for nothing, and that the parts of it fit one into another in some way; and that the world goes on, beautiful and strange and dreadful and worshipful" [Morris Letters, I, 291].

At the same time he wrote to Aglaia. "I am getting on with my poem, in quantity at any rate," he told her. "I have (roughly) done the 3rd part [of four]: that is Sigurd & Brynhild are dead, & people are busy forgetting them after the fashion of our aimiable [sic] race: all that I have left to do now, if the last written parts turn out successful, is the revenge and death of Gudrun, which will be certainly short, and probably not difficult compared with what I have had to do" [Mackail, I, 327-8].

The end of March 1876 was another key moment in Morris's life. As he completed his forty-second year and the third part of *Sigurd*, Morris put romance aside and ceased to be the idle singer of an empty day.

Chapter Thirteen

Do you know them? - Greedy gamblers on the Stock Exchange

With the completion of *Sigurd the Volsung* in 1876 William Morris reawakened his conscience, sublimated his obsession and directed its energy from writing erotic poetry to promoting social transformation. Morris had always preferred the antique to the new, the authentic to the contrived and the essential to the merely decorative. Entering the era of his maturity, he wished for nothing less than to shape the structure and conscience of his country through the metaphor of its architecture and the thrust of its politics.

His interest in architecture began early. As a child he went on many visits to local churches with his father, culminating in their dramatic journey to Canterbury in 1842. Though his formal training in the field lasted less than a year, he studied ecclesiastical architecture throughout his life and valued the artistic accomplishments of medieval builders. He hated most modern development. He especially deplored what he saw as the depredation of old churches in the name of restoration.

The idea of starting an organization to combat this barbaric destruction first occurred to him in Leek when he and Wardle visited Lichfield Cathedral, which was undergoing just such a restoration. Shortly after, in early September 1876, while visiting his old Oxford friend Cormel Price in the Cotswolds, he stopped at Burford. He was horrified by the alterations underway on the parish church. Before returning to London, he wrote the first draft of a statement outlining the formation of the Society for the Protection of Ancient Buildings, better known as Anti-Scrape.

Morris believed that contemporary architects were ignorant of history, partly because the nineteenth century, unlike earlier periods, had developed no style of its own. Architecture had fallen into a kind of un-rooted vacuum. Preservationists had no idea how to repair an ancient building.

> Those who make the changes wrought in our day under the name of Restoration, while professing to bring back a building to the best time of its history, have no guide but each his own individual whim to point out to them what is admirable and what contemptible, while the very nature of their task compels them to destroy something and to supply the gap by imagining what the earlier builders should or might have done. [Morris Letters, I, 360]

The result, he asserted, was a forgery. The aim of Anti-Scrape was to prevent radical surgery and unnecessary alteration. It would promote care and maintenance, in other words genuine preservation.

Before he could get Anti-Scrape off the ground, Morris was struck by the news that England was on the verge of war with Russia. For centuries England had fretted over the expansion of Russia. Its search for warm-water ports and trade routes threatened England's interests in the eastern Mediterranean and beyond. The tension between the two nations erupted when Turkish forces massacred Bulgarian civilians in the Balkans.

England supported Turkey as a bulwark against Russian encroachments. Russia backed the aspirations of the Bulgarians in their effort to win independence from Turkish control. Within England public opinion was sharply divided. Many approved of the tough stance taken by the Tory government, which threatened Russia with war. Others, like Morris, sympathized with the victims in Bulgaria.

Until now Morris had played no active role in politics, but his first venture was a dramatic one. He sent a bristling, combative letter to the *Daily News*, and it appeared in the issue for the 24 October 1876. Oblivious to geopolitical interests, Morris felt that the target of England's wrath should be Turkey, not Russia. The matter was plain. The Turks, "who, to speak the downright truth, are a gang of thieves and murderers." They denied the Bulgarians, "who are quite orderly and industrious," the chance for "some security for life, limb, and property." Calling himself "a mere sentimentalist," he attacked the Tories as unreconstructed mercenaries. He appealed to men of conscience (members of the Liberal party, working-men, and the large body of "quiet men" like himself) to set England straight. He signed the letter "William Morris, Author of *The Earthly Paradise*" [Morris Letters, I, 323, 326].

He was invited shortly after to join a committee to resist the Tory government's pro-Turkish, anti-Russian foreign policy. The committee organized a national conference that was held on 8 December 1876 and attracted 700 people. Morris sat among the notables, which included Charles Darwin, John Ruskin, Robert Browning, Anthony Trollope and the principal speaker, William Gladstone, the former Liberal Prime Minister. Gladstone gripped the audience with his vociferous denunciations of Turk and Tory. At the end of the conference the committee formalized itself as the Eastern Question Association (EQA) to carry on the work of opposition. Morris was elected treasurer.

Joined with the EQA to fight political oppression abroad, he presented his plan to combat architectural destruction at home. He wrote to *The Athenaeum* on 5 March 1877,

> My eye just now caught the word 'restoration' in the morning paper, and, on looking closer, I saw that this time it is nothing less than the Minster of Tewkesbury that is to be destroyed by Sir Gilbert Scott.

Morris saw Scott, the foremost restorer of churches in England, as the chief villain. He declared that it was now time to establish an organization

> to keep a watch on old monuments, to protest against all 'restoration' that means more than keeping out wind and weather, and, by all means, literary and other, to awaken a feeling that our ancient buildings are not mere ecclesiastical toys, but sacred monuments of the nation's growth and hope. [Morris Letters, I, 351-2]

Having stated his position publicly, he began recruiting his friends and acquaintances. Anti-Scrape held its first meeting in early April 1877 with

Morris serving as first secretary. The group acted quickly. It launched an attack on Sir Gilbert Scott's plan to rip out the choir in Canterbury Cathedral. Church officials wanted Scott to replace the seventeenth-century choir with a nineteenth-century copy of the twelfth-century original. In a letter to *The Times* (4 June 1877) Morris observed that, though the choir itself was a restoration, it was serviceable, dignified and beautiful, and should be left untouched. Moreover no one knew what the original looked like. The idea of making unnecessary changes based solely on conjecture was totally irresponsible. He warned that if Gilbert Scott had his way,

> we shall see the noble building of the two Williams [Kings William I and II] confused and falsified by the usual mass of ecclesiastical trumpery and coarse daubing that all true lovers of art and history dread so sorely.

He predicted the beauty of Canterbury would suffer just like all the other church projects undertaken by Scott [Morris Letters, I, 374-5]. Despite his warning, Scott's work went ahead as planned.

In the meantime, on 24 April 1877, Russia declared war on Turkey. Fearful that England would react by going to war against Russia, Morris published on 11 May a manifesto entitled *Unjust War.* The manifesto was more intense and sharply focused than his letter to the *Daily News* six months earlier. He no longer appealed to the liberal and quiet men of his own class, but addressed himself directly to "The Working-men of England." The manifesto was in fact an incitement to class action. Employing the polemic devices of rhetorical question, stereotyping and sarcasm he asked,

> Who are they that are leading us into war?. . . Do you know them? – Greedy gamblers on the Stock Exchange, idle officers of the army and navy (poor fellows!), worn-out mockers of the Clubs, desperate purveyors of exciting war-news for the comfortable breakfast-tables of those who have nothing to lose by war. [Morris Letters H, 358]

His shift in focus and change in tone reflected his closer acquaintance with working class leaders. Through the EQA he met Henry Broadhurst and Thomas Burt, who impressed him with their force of character and sense of justice. They were members of the Labour Representative League (LRL), which sought to elect workingmen to parliament as Liberal Party candidates. Burt, a coal miner from Northumberland, had won a seat in the House of Commons in 1874 and would be continually re-elected until 1922. Morris met him for the first time on 2 May (nine days before he issued *Unjust War*) at a working men's meeting held to support several resolutions sponsored by Gladstone. Burt chaired the meeting and gave an "excellent" though short speech, delivered with a strong Northumbrian accent. Morris thought him, without irony, "a capital fellow" [Morris Letters, I, 370].

Morris especially wanted his readers to see inside the capitalist heart. He wrote in *Unjust War*,

> I doubt if you know the bitterness of hatred against freedom and progress that lies at the hearts of a certain part of the richer classes in this country, Their newspapers veil it in a kind of decent language; but do but hear them talking among themselves, as I have often, and I know not whether scorn or anger would prevail in you at their folly and insolence.

He warned that the consequences of war (higher taxes, higher prices, and especially military casualties and deaths) would hit the working class the hardest. The fact was that the governing class of England, he continued, understands nothing and cares nothing for working class interests. Just like the Turks, whom they supported,

> these men, if they had the power (may England perish rather!), would thwart your just aspirations, would silence you, would deliver you bound hand and foot for ever to irresponsible capital – and these men, I say it deliberately, are the heart and soul of the party that is driving us to an unjust war.

The logic of his argument led Morris to a novel conclusion. Moral leadership could come only from the working class. He admonished working men to cry out against injustice, and to "urge us of the Middle Classes to do no less" [Morris Letters H, 388-9].

Morris spoke from his own experience. As a director of the Devon

Great Consolidated Copper Mining Company he collected £100 a year for a perfunctory service. As the company began to fail in the early 1870s the directors maintained their stipends while they cut benefits for the education of the miners' children. At the annual meeting of the company in May 1874 a stockholder, Mr. Taylor, asked how many children were affected. There were four board directors at the meeting: W.A. Thomas, the chairman, J. Blackwell, Thomas Morris and William Morris. Speaking for the board, Thomas Morris said that there were between fifty and sixty children. Mr. Taylor observed that, "the sum appeared small for the promotion of the education of that number of children." Mr. Morris explained that

> when the company was in a better position the annual vote was 100 guineas [£105], but lately it had been reduced to 30 guineas, of which 20 where given to the school and 10 to the dispensary.

Another shareholder "hoped the time was not far distant when the vote would be increased to 100 guineas." Mr. Thomas, the chairman, responded that, "the directors would not be found illiberal in that respect when the financial condition of the company justified" [*The Mining Journal,* 30 May 1874, p. 549].

Several days before this meeting, Morris had written to his mother to say that he was about to meet with his brother Arthur regarding the upcoming board meeting. His mind was focused on sales, fees and dividends. Responding to her apparent concern about the company's financial health, he told her,

> I don't know what may happen at the meeting, but think that nothing will be done: things are looking a little better there, & the last sale was (comparatively) good as I daresay you have heard. [Morris Letters, I, 223]

As an investor he naturally thought of his own interests before those of the men who actually mined the copper ore. He knew from his own heart how self-interest can chill a man's conscience.

His experiences and his insights stirred him to think more deeply about the connection between art and politics. Like other Victorians, he believed in progress, but unlike most he did not think it resulted from advances in technology. Nor did he think that improvement was general and steady. Real advances came in human relations with the expansion of liberty and a sense of responsibility. In England the political revolution of the seventeenth century and the emergence of Oliver Cromwell, whom Morris saw as a great leader of the common man, represented the high mark. Since then the nation had declined. The steam engine, the railroad and the factory system had made matters worse. Social classes were more divided as wealth became concentrated into fewer hands. The division was reflected in the arts. In his first public lecture, delivered before the Trades Guild of Learning in London on 4 December 1877, Morris told his audience that the divorce between the lesser and greater arts was "a bad symptom" of the times.

He defined the greater arts as architecture, painting and sculpture, and the lesser or decorative arts as carpentry, metalworking, pottery, weaving, dying, and glassmaking. He observed that in times past the lesser and greater arts were closely and productively allied, but in modern times they had separated. The split proved baleful for both. The greater lost "their dignity of popular arts, and became nothing but dull adjuncts to unnecessary pomp, or ingenious toys for a few rich and idle men." The lesser, falling victim to fashion and deceit, became mechanical and trivial. Everyone was at fault. All classes of society preferred money before nature. Echoing Carlyle and Ruskin, he adapted a Biblical voice:

> Is money to be gathered? Cut down the pleasant trees among the houses, pull down ancient and venerable buildings for the money that a few square yards of London dirt will fetch; blacken rivers, hide the sun and poison the air with smoke and worse, and it's nobody's business to see to it or mend it. [Morris, XXIII, 5-24]

He argued that the arts could not be made whole until the body politic regained its health. A healthy society had to be in tune with nature and in harmony with itself. For this to happen, all members of society had to participate at all levels and in every way. "I do not want art for the few, any more than education for a few, or freedom for a few." It was most important, he thought, that everyone see that work is a blessing, not a curse, for all proper work was in effect a form of art. The goodness of work was revealed in the optimal intersect between maker and user.

> To give people pleasure in the things they must perforce *use*, that is the just office of decoration; to give people pleasure in the things they must perforce *make*, that is the other use.

Good work was beautiful, useful and natural to both the worker and the user.

> The hand of the Craftsman, is guided to work in the way [nature] does, till the web, the cup, or the knife, look as natural, nay as lovely, as the green field, the river bank, or the mountain flint [Morris, XXIII, 5-24].

Morris followed his first formal lecture with his first public speech six weeks later. For most of the year war fever stayed at a high pitch. Then, on 18 January 1878, just as hostilities seemed certain, Morris addressed a large audience in Exeter Hall, a meeting jointly sponsored by the EQA and the LRL. He spoke well. The crowd cheered him when he talked in favor of peace and groaned when he alluded to the Tories. The chairman had to admonish him for referring directly to the Queen as his enthusiasm carried him along. Queen Victoria was known to be anti-Russian, but it was against etiquette to mention the monarch's name in a public speech. Writing to Janey, who had taken Jenny and May to Italy for the winter, he expressed his overall satisfaction and enjoyment:

> The evening meeting was magnificent: orderly and enthusiastic; though mind you, it took some very heavy work to keep the enemies roughs out; and the noise of them outside was like the sea roaring against a lighthouse. [Morris Letters, I, 435]

A few days after, he learned that the government had sent the British fleet to the Dardenelles. He and members of the EQA and LRL called on Gladstone who agreed to make another open speech at the end of February in a final effort to avoid a war. Morris rented the Agricultural Hall, the largest in London, just as the news broke that the Russians had entered Constantinople. The threat to England's national interests overwhelmed any thought of maintaining neutrality. The Liberals in Parliament began to prevaricate and pressure Gladstone to back off. Morris was unprepared when the EQA itself caved in. He did not blame Gladstone who, he told Janey on 20 February 1878, "was quite ready to come up to the scratch & has behaved well throughout." As for himself, he was so ashamed that he could "scarcely look people in the face though I did my best to keep the thing up." He felt particularly badly about letting down the working men, who he believed, were "in a great rage" over the retreat. Thoroughly disgusted, he decided that he had enough of politics. He told her,

> I am out of it now, I mean as to bothering my head about it: I shall give up reading the Papers, and shall stick to my work [Morris Letters, I, 450].

It was just as well as the Russians and Turks stopped fighting and signed a peace agreement on 3 March 1878 at San Stefano.

Morris did stay out of it for a while, but he continued to think. He did not yet have a clear vision about how progress might resume, how art and the body politic might be made whole again. He thought it would require a drastic change of some sort. In his lecture he spoke of wiping the slate clean. When change occurs, he said, it will come quickly: "it will be but a burning up of the gathered weeds, so that the field may bear more abundantly" [Morris, XXIII, 22]. Four months later, however, he reached a clear and pointed conclusion. Wardle sent him a copy of a lecture that Matthew Arnold delivered in February 1878 on the subject of equality. Arnold argued that social inequality in England was the result of the ancient laws of inheritance. Morris read the text and told Wardle that he agreed, but lamented that Arnold offered no solution. So he provided his own. He wrote to Wardle on 8 March 1878,

> I think myself that no rose-water will cure us, disaster & misfortune of all kinds, I think will be the only things that will breed a remedy: in short nothing can be done till all rich men are made poor by common consent. [Morris Letters, I, 454]

Chapter Fourteen

They lie in prison for it, work in mines, are exiled, and ruined for it

Five years before he discovered Karl Marx, Morris divined that the rich had to be dispossessed to make society whole and wholesome again. He believed that radical change was the only solution, but he could not see how it would happen.

He drifted for a while in the early 1880s. War with Russia had been avoided. Morris & Co. prospered and expanded. The protests of Anti-Scrape were usually ignored. The Liberals were fractious and seemed not much different from the Tories on the important issues of imperialism and poverty. Working class leaders appeared distracted, clueless and deferential. He wrote in a New Year's letter in 1880,

> I am in rather a discouraged mood, and the whole thing seems almost too tangled to see through and too heavy to move. Happily though, I am not bound either to see through it or move it but a very little way: meantime I do know what I love and what I hate, and believe that neither the love nor the hatred are matters of accident or whim. [Mackail, II, 23]

He accepted the contradiction in his being a capitalist advocate for social change, though sometimes he became angry with himself. While much of what his company produced met his own criteria of satisfying both maker and user, his products were out of reach of all but the most affluent. He wondered whether he was doing anything more than merely amusing himself: "Am I doing nothing but make-believe then, something like Louis XVI's lock-making?" [Morris Letters, II, 95]. Once he turned "like a wild animal" on one of his wealthy clients, and told him that he lost his temper because "I spend my life in ministering to the swinish luxury of the rich" [Webb, 94]. The Firm in fact made nothing that fit with his notion of plain living. He told William Butler Yeats not long after they first met,

> I decorate modern houses for people, but the house that would please me would be some great room where one talked to one's friends in one corner, and ate in another, and slept in another, and worked in another. [*Fortnightly Review*, March 1903, p. 539]

In a lecture in 1881, he said

> Simplicity of life, even the barest, is not a misery, but the very foundation of refinement: a sanded floor and white-washed walls, and the green trees and flowery meads and living waters outside. [Morris, XXII, 150]

In July 1881 he was shaken by the announcement that Johann Most had been sentenced to sixteen months in prison. Most, the German editor of a socialist newspaper printed in England, had written an article praising the assassination of Alexander II, the tsar of Russia. The Liberal government charged Most for encouraging the murderers, even though the article was written after the fact. Morris, who did not know Most, found the verdict outrageous. It destroyed any lingering faith he still had in gradual progress. The verdict was the sort of thing, he told Georgie Burne-Jones, that makes

> thinking people so sick at heart that they are driven from all interest in politics save revolutionary politics: which I must say seems like to be my case.

He told her that he had known for a long time that modern society "was founded on injustice and kept together by cowardice and tyranny," but that he had trusted that "matters would mend gradually, till the last struggle." He thought the final struggle, though "mingled with violence, and madness," would be "so short as scarcely to count" [Morris Letters, II, 51]. Now he implied that revolution might be long and possibly bloody.

Gripped by the sentence imposed on Most, Morris decided to join a socialist party. At first there was no single, discernible body of consequence for him to join. The socialist stew in London in the early 1880s was a heady mix of former Chartists, radicals, trade unionists, refugees, and alienated members of the middle class operating in small and scattered groups.

The very definition of socialism was kaleidoscopic. Instead of joining a group, he read. During 1882 he read four books that moved his imagination forward: More's *Utopia*, Butler's *Erewhon,* George's *Progress and Poverty* and Wallace's *Land Nationalization.* He may also have read, or at least begun, Marx's *Capital.* Towards the end of the year he met Henry Hyndman, who invited him to join the Democratic Federation.

Morris accepted Hyndman's overture on the expectation that the organization would declare for socialism. The Democratic Federation was formed in 1881, and Hyndman had assumed its leadership from the beginning. Like Morris, Hyndman was middle class, wealthy and well educated (at Cambridge). He was also a little younger, but equally energetic, more autocratic and less comfortable with working men. He had read *Capital* in 1880, met Marx and was ready for socialism. He believed that the coming revolution would happen first in England and would happen soon. Morris was satisfied and signed his membership card on 13 January 1883 as "William Morris, designer."

He entered the Democratic Federation with enthusiasm. He told Hyndman that he would do whatever he was asked. At one of his first meetings he was struck by the idea of taking socialism directly to the street. Practiced in speaking to groups indoors, he was eager to face larger audiences outdoors and talk of social revolution. In his speeches Morris said less about goals (public education, decent housing, progressive taxation and collective ownership of the means of production) than he did about sacrifice. To many people the goals seemed absurd and out of reach, but socialism for Morris was

> a cause that men and women would die for. They lie in prison for it, work in mines, are exiled, are ruined for it: believe me when such things are suffered for dreams, the dreams come true at last.

Allegiance to the cause required sacrifice, the sacrifice of "leisure, pleasure and money, each according to his means." It also meant sacrificing one's individuality to the organization for "without organization the cause *is* but a vague dream" [May Morris, II, 403-4].

Morris himself sacrificed a lot. He took time away from the Firm to give to the cause. He put up money, and so was elected Treasurer of the Federation. Out of the closet of middle-class respectability he jeopardized his reputation as an artist and poet. Friends began to shy away, though he persuaded a few, like Webb and Faulkner, to embrace socialism. He endured a "storm of newspaper brickbats" for appearing inconsistent. To some he replied. In a letter written to *The Standard* in response to one such complainant he gave an eloquent and compelling explanation of an apparent but insubstantial contradiction. He wrote to the newspaper on 23 November 1883,

> Your Correspondent, implies that to be consistent we should at once cast aside our position of capitalists, and take rank with the proletariat; but he must excuse my saying that he knows very well we are not able to do so; that the most we can do is to palliate as far as we can the evils of the unjust system which we are forced to sustain; that we are but minute links in the immense chain of the terrible organization of competitive commerce, and that only the complete unrivetting of that chain will really free us.

Ineffective as individuals, he argued that people like himself were drawn to take an active role in a movement whose final success "will deprive us of our capitalist position." The sacrifice, he asserted, would be worth the trouble, because everyone will "receive in return gifts which no money can buy." Morris looked forward to the end of poverty as well as riches and the end of squalor as well as luxury. The end result of socialism was to be the creation of leisure, pleasure, and refinement for everyone, including those "who do the rough work of the world." This would lead to the reemergence of a "healthy art growing spontaneously from this happiness" [Morris Letters, II, 248].

Morris was prepared to sacrifice a lot, but he hedged on his willingness to sacrifice for the organization. When he was made treasurer in May 1883, he realized that he was taking on more work. But he also felt queasy about Hyndman's leadership. Hyndman was imperious and condescending, given to intrigue, and Morris was afraid, not always honest. He worried in particular that Hyndman was moving too fast, trying to force or, worse, threaten a revolution before the working class was adequately educated for the task. By August he found himself drifting into the uncongenial role of "moderator and patcher up" [Mackail, II, 111]. Despite his efforts to maintain a center of gravity, the rift between the two capitalist executives of the socialist organization widened. By the following August Morris could see the end, which finally came in December after he made a disastrous trip to Scotland.

Morris went to Scotland to lecture and to foster cooperation between two new socialist groups in Edinburgh and Glasgow. The group based in Glasgow was organized as a branch of the now Social-Democratic Federation (SDF); the other, in Edinburgh, was formed as an affiliate under the banner of the Scottish Land and Labour League. Hyndman played the principal role in setting up the branch in Glasgow. Andreas Scheu, another member of the SDF executive board, was instrumental in getting the Edinburgh affiliate off the ground. Between Hyndman and Scheu there lay a deep strain of animosity. Both men were proud and contentious, each convinced that he knew more Marxian theory than the other. Hyndman disdained Scheu as a refugee (from Germany) and an anarchist. Morris found Scheu knowledgeable, dedicated and hardworking.

After speaking to a small group in a private clubroom in Edinburgh on 13 December 1884 and a large audience of about 3,000 in Glasgow the following day, Morris went across town to the warehouse district to meet with members of the new branch. He knew there was disagreement among them about whether or not to accept co-operation with the Edinburgh affiliate, but he did not expect the frigid greeting he received from the branch Secretary, W.J. Nairne. Morris spoke briefly about common goals and working together and then invited questions. John Bruce Glasier, a young architectural draftsman and ultimately a great admirer of Morris, attended the meeting and remembered that Nairne immediately began to heckle Morris as if he were an enemy. Morris maintained his calm and responded to the questions with good humor. When the questions ended and he rose to leave, Nairne threw one more dart: "Does Comrade Morris accept Marx's theory of value?" Finally vexed Morris shot back,

> I am asked if I believe in Marx's theory of value. To speak quite frankly, I do not know what Marx's theory of value is, and I'm damned if I want to know.

He went on to say that he tried to study Marx, but political economy was not his strength. It was enough to know that "the idle class is rich and the working class is poor, and that the rich are rich because they rob the poor." It was not necessary to read books to see the obvious or to be a socialist. The main point, he insisted, is that "the whole system is monstrous and intolerable, and what we Socialists have got to do is to work together" [Glasier, 31-2].

Morris was not pleased. He deduced that Hyndman put Nairne up to making trouble, and was ready to have it out with him. He wrote after the fact.

> The spectacle of the discord so deliberately sown among these new recruits fairly swept away all doubt in my mind as to what was necessary to be done, I saw that the dispute *must* come off, and that it must be fought on the true grounds, namely resistance to H's absolutism. [May Morris, II, 589]

On his return to London he gathered his forces and assessed his position. He calculated that he had the necessary votes to force Hyndman to step down. He rejoiced at the thought of victory (he would not have to shake his hand again), but then realized that Hyndman would remain a member and continue to create dissension. He decided it was not worth fighting and persuaded his supporters to resign. Hyndman could keep the Federation and

> frighten the Government, which I really think is about all his scheme; and we will begin again quite clean-handed to try the more humdrum method of quiet propaganda,

he wrote to Georgie Burne-Jones on Christmas Eve, 1884 [Morris Letters, II, 353]. Four days later he rented office space for a new organization.

Chapter Fifteen

We got pleasure into our work; then we became conscious of that pleasure

The Socialist League was formally organized on 30 December 1884 at 27 Farringdon Street, London. The twenty-three members who constituted the League's Provisional Council were mostly men who left the SDF with Morris. They appointed Morris treasurer and editor of the League's newspaper, which they called the *Commonweal*. Morris consulted with Engels and accepted his recommendation that the paper come out monthly rather than weekly to concentrate content and keep down costs. The first issue, which appeared on the first of February, was a smashing success, selling 5,000 copies and going into a second edition. The second issue, released in March, was even more noteworthy, and included an editorial and a poem by Morris, articles by George Bernard Shaw and Karl Marx's daughter, Eleanor, and Engel's learned piece on "England in 1845 and in 1885."

Officially the League advocated "the principles of Revolutionary International Socialism," which meant, according to its manifesto, the eradication of "the distinctions of classes and nationalities" around the world. At first the members proposed adoption of a number of specific points as an official platform. One goal, which implicitly condemned the recent split, called for drawing all socialists into a unified party. Others included running candidates for political offices and promoting the formation of labor unions. The proposed goals were never approved in large part because Morris opposed them. He felt that they were distractions from the main task.

Morris envisaged a violent revolution to break down the class system. He did not imagine that the rich and powerful would concede control merely for the asking. So he thought working for palliatives (like working class representation, better wages, shorter hours) through parliamentary action and union activities was a loser's game. The rich were smart enough to co-opt workers with small concessions, without ever relinquishing real power or property. But he was also convinced that a successful revolution required solid leaders and would not come about just because a large majority wished it. In his first interview as the founder of the Socialist League, he re-iterated the importance of education. He told the *Daily News* (8 January 1885) that, since the old order could be overthrown only by force, it was necessary that the revolution be guided by intelligence, not ignorance. He said,

> What I should like to have now, far more than anything else, would be a body of able, high-minded, competent men, who should act as instructors of the masses and as their leaders during critical periods of the movement.

He thought most of these instructors and organizers should be working men. He wanted 2,000 men teaching the tenets of "rational, scientific Socialism all over the kingdom" [Thompson, 379].

The goal was commendable but out of reach; the initial enthusiasm and surge of interest in the League soon dissolved. By May, Morris found himself "in low spirits about the prospects of our 'party,' if I can dignify a little knot of men by such a word" [Mackail, II, 144]. The numbers of converts refused to grow, despite his efforts. After its first appearance, *Commonweal* continued to sell for a while from 2,000 to 3,000 copies an issue but Morris could not gather 2,000 able-bodied, high-minded, competent men to organize and teach. At its height in 1885-87 the Socialist League may have numbered as many as 700 members, only a fraction of whom met his criteria of competency. Outsiders were indifferent, dubious or horrified by socialism. Those within the socialist circle were divided, not just between the Federation and the League, but also among the pragmatists who wanted better conditions and a parliamentary presence, the anarchists who wanted to tear everything down and the purists, like Morris, who wanted to concentrate on education. On top of that, the authorities began to crack down. In September 1885 several open-air speakers were arrested. When they were brought to court the following morning Morris and other members of the League attended to protest against the charges. He was nearly arrested for disorderly conduct, but was released when he responded to the magistrate's question, "What are you?" by saying, "I am an artist and literary man, pretty well known, I think, throughout Europe" [Mackail, II, 147]. News of the prosecutions gave the cause a momentary lift but embarrassed Morris. The working men went to jail, and the respectable poet and middle-class socialist got to go home.

A few weeks later, in October, Morris succumbed to a severe attack of gout and remained crippled and out of action for more than a month. Georgie Burne-Jones, who was always interested in what Morris did and thought, apparently urged him to ease up his activities. He told her that he couldn't. It was "a matter of duty." He had to do "what I can while I last." He acknowledged that even in an organization dedicated to absolute freedom "some sort of leadership is required" and that he unfortunately supplied the need. He also admitted that he was obsessed:

> You see, my dear, I can't help it. The ideas which have taken hold of me will not let me rest: nor can I see anything else worth thinking of.

He saw the world in a way that ordinary people, fixed in their culture, could never see. He added,

> How can it be otherwise, when to me society, which to many seems an orderly arrangement for allowing decent people to get through their lives creditably and with some pleasure, seems mere cannibalism. [Mackail, II, 149-50]

Daunted by the daily grind of leadership and the difficulty of getting his educational message across, Morris found more satisfaction, if not greater success, in the three socialist romances that he wrote during his years at the League. In these highly imaginary tales he drew out of himself his clearest visualization of socialism present, past and future. In each he gave himself a central role as actor and observer. All were designed to be educational. The first was a long narrative poem entitled

The Pilgrims of Hope, which appeared in serial form between April 1885 and June 1886 in *Commonweal*.

The story begins twenty years earlier. The hopeful pilgrims are two young men and a woman who fight for a better world. Richard comes from a modest country family. His father left him a small inheritance, which has somehow slipped away, and he faces making a life for himself as a carpenter in London. He marries, has a son, joins a socialist group, begins to proselytize at work and gets fired. He speaks at an open-air meeting, thrashes a heckler and goes to prison for two months. The magistrate claims that English society provides a pathway for men with talent. Since Richard is bright and capable he should keep his opinions to himself, work hard and maybe some day find success as a small house builder. Out of prison, Richard makes a friend, Arthur, a gentleman who shares his dream of better days and gives him work as a writer. Arthur meets and falls in love with Richard's wife. Momentary feelings of betrayal and embarrassment are eclipsed by the news that Paris has fallen to the Communards. Richard leaves his son in the care of a friend, and the gallant trio goes to France to join the revolution. They are ground up by the brutal bourgeois war-machine. Richard is wounded, and his wife and Arthur are killed. Richard returns to London having learned the hard lessons of fighting without clear plans or proper organization. Discouraged but not defeated, he vows that he and his son will continue the good fight against capitalist oppression.

In February 1886, a few months before Morris completed *The Pilgrims of Hope*, a gathering of unemployed men in Trafalgar Square led to a riot that caused some property damage and shattered nerves. The mob nearly ransacked the Firm's store in Oxford Street before the police finally dispersed it. Morris deplored the riot, calling it a revolutionary incident without purpose or aim. "At the risk of being misunderstood by hot-heads," he wrote in *Commonweal*, "I say that our business is more than ever *Education*." The hot-heads were mainly the anarchist members of the League whom he was trying, with increasing difficulty, to keep in line. In his editorial he asked them to consider the consequences of an aimless revolt. Suppose it were successful, led by "a small number of men capable of government and administration, though that is supposing a great deal." Then what? Without clear aims and a mass of working men educated to those aims, the revolt would fail. Counter-revolution would sweep them all away in an instant, as it did the Communards in Paris in 1870 [Mackail, II, 153]. Unwilling to support the opportunistic goals of the pragmatic elements in the socialist movement and hostile to the hot-heads, Morris found himself isolated even as he tried to hold everyone together. "It is a tough job," he admitted, "something like the worst kind of pig-driving I should think, and sometimes I lose my temper over it" [Mackail, II, 184-5].

Concerned about the need for solidarity, organization and inspirational leadership, Morris began *A Dream of John Ball*, which ran in the League's magazine from November 1886 through February 1887. For this story he went back five hundred years. He imagined that he had woken up in Kent in the year 1381, the time of the Peasants' Revolt. He finds himself among a gathering of men preparing to defend themselves against an army of the lords who would beat them down and cast them into servitude. The yeomen are stout and brave men. They are well armed and inspired by their leader, the preacher John Ball, who appeals to their sense of fellowship. With superior skill, better disposition of forces and right on their side, the farmers drive the enemy from the field. Afterwards Morris has a long conversation with Ball about the future. Ball is a medieval socialist. He sees a day when

> all men shall work and none make to work, and so shall none be robbed, and at last shall all men labour and live and be happy, and have the goods of the earth without money and without price. [Morris, XVI, 270]

Morris tells Ball that it will take more than five hundred years for his dream to come true. Talking through the night, he describes conditions in the nineteenth century to Ball's indignation and sometimes incomprehension. When Ball begins to despair about the future, Morris assures him that his dream will come true.

If Morris still harbored hopes of an imminent and successful revolution when he finished the story of John Ball, he was soon disabused. The denouement came late in the year of the Queen's Jubilee, which celebrated fifty years of Victorian rule in 1887. On 13 November, a huge crowd composed mainly of unemployed working class men marched on

Trafalgar Square to oppose the government's harsh and unyielding policy against the Home Rule movement in Ireland, and to assert the right to free speech and assembly. Planned and announced in advance, the size and character of the demonstration alarmed the authorities. They feared that it might lead to a popular insurrection. Police and military forces charged the crowd of thousands creating a great deal of confusion and fear. Within a few hours they quelled the demonstration and re-gained control of the streets. Morris, who led a contingent carrying the banner of the Socialist League, witnessed the clash and recorded how the police, unprovoked and brutal, attacked the marchers as if they were an enemy. A few men were killed, and hundreds were injured and arrested during the melee that ensued.

For Morris Bloody Sunday was a heavy blow, though he was not entirely surprised by the sorry results. The event proved what he already knew: that the socialists and the working class were grossly unprepared. It nettled him that working men resisted revolutionary education in favor of tangible benefits (a few hours off the working week, a few extra pence an hour, a few more working class candidates elected to city councils and parliament). He confessed that his purism might be a bit precious, but pragmatism represented capitulation and made him sick. Most of all he was outraged that the larger good could be so easily beaten by the smaller evil.

Nearly three years passed between the conclusion of his second socialist tale (*A Dream of John Ball* in February 1887) and the beginning of the third (*News from Nowhere* in January 1890). In the intervening period he wrote two other stories. Both reach back to early periods in European history and record the efforts of small social groups fighting to preserve their independence and communal way of life. In *A Tale of the House of the Wolfings and All the Kindreds of the Mark*, begun and completed in 1888, the families of the Mark are threatened by the encroachment of an expanding Roman empire. In *The Roots of the Mountain*, begun and completed in 1889, the Burgdalers help the Mountain folk regain their home ground, taken from them by the Felons. Both books are about fierce and bloody fighting ending in triumph. The victors, smaller in number, retain or regain what is rightfully theirs. Their success comes from the critical elements that Morris found missing among the socialist groups and the working class: courage, co-ordination, military know-how and strength of purpose. In the first book the men of the Mark win despite the sudden impotence of their leader; Thiodolf faints in battle, not once but twice, at critical moments. Even so they drive off the Romans. It is easy to imagine Morris investing his feelings of inadequacy in his description of Thiodolf's collapses.

In 1888-89 his grip on the Socialist League slipped. New interests developed as he wrote *The House* and *The Book*. He decided to develop his own type for printing his books. Soon he thought to print and publish his books, and those of favored authors such as Chaucer and Ruskin. He continued to speak, lecture and proselytize. In the meantime most of the stronger and more pro-active members left to join the Fabian Society or re-join the SDF, leaving him stranded with the anarchist rump. In May 1889 the hot-heads finally gained control of the League and took over the editorship of *Commonweal*. Morris, who founded, financed and embodied the League, was put aside. He did not withdraw immediately but continued to provide substantial, though now reduced, monetary support. In 1890 he made his biggest contribution to the cause in writing *News from Nowhere* (from January to October) in the pages of *Commonweal*.

In this third and last of his socialist romances, Morris imagined himself waking one day after an evening of vigorous debate at the League about the future of society. It is a hot summer morning. As he goes out his front door he decides to enjoy a dip in the Thames. A young man parked in a boat meant for bathers takes him out into mid-stream where he strips and jumps into the surprisingly clear river. After his swim, the boatman rows him upstream where Morris begins to notice that the riverscape is different from the day before. The soap-works and the lead-works are gone; the air is bright and pure, and he is stunned by the silence. There is no racket of riveting, hammering or steam engines. And here is a bridge he hasn't seen before, more delightful than the Ponte Vecchio. "Is it old?" he asks. No, it is not old at all. It was built in 2003.

In *News from Nowhere* Morris brings us into a brave new world where the adults are healthy and beautiful while the children are talented and independent. Everyone is civil and productive. Leisure is found in work, for all work is enjoyable as well as useful. Farming, gardening, house-building, street-paving and domestic chores are amusing and popular social activities. The best-dressed man in town is the garbage man and why not? It is what he likes. Everyone else is dressed in plain, comfortable clothes. Since work is plentiful and pleasant, everything in the marketplace is free. There is no need for money, so there is none. Government too has ceased to exist. The Houses of Parliament serve as an extension of the market and a storage place for manure. Poverty has lapsed from the vocabulary, and the word 'poor' refers only to those who are ailing. Wealth, power, property rights and social discord have evaporated. So have machines (except for truly irksome work). Real work is done by hand, and the amount of work and the number of workers always match. There is never any "difficulty in finding work that suits the special turn of mind of everybody; so that no man is sacrificed to the wants of another," and everything wanted is produced and made available [Morris, XVI, 97]. Visible hands magically guide economic activity in the socialist paradise.

In his dream-visit to the future Morris learns from old Hammond how the change came about. In the late nineteenth century economic conditions were deplorable. A group of far-sighted men, known as socialists, envisaged a brighter future and engaged to convey their vision to the downtrodden working class. Yet even they or at least most of them despaired of the difficulty in explaining something so beautiful and simple to a large number whose minds were focused on making ends meet at the end of each day. Instead they turned their attention to the more immediate aim of trying to ameliorate the pain of working class men and women. Amelioration helped to ease their burden, but more importantly it awakened the workers to a clearer awareness of their oppression. Over time and after many setbacks they learned how to combine into a federation for greater effectiveness in their struggle. They were able to press the government to pass regulations to enforce fewer hours in the working week and higher pay. Eventually they established state-owned factories. This movement toward state socialism went a long way to undermine the commercial practices of the property-owning class and brought the country to the edge of economic collapse.

In the year 1952 the Combined Workers, watching as the nation teetered, decided to serve the government with an ultimatum to turn all the country's natural resources and their management over to the workers and to render the wealthy class into a ward of the state. The ultimatum was received, as it was intended, as a declaration of class war. The rich prevailed on the government to take action to "repress the insatiable greed of the lower classes." A series of confrontations led to a major encounter in Trafalgar Square in which the army fired into the giant crowd, killing between one and two thousand mostly unarmed workers.

At this point in the narrative Morris assumes, thinking of his own experience in Trafalgar Square on Bloody Sunday, that the massacre put a stop to the incipient revolution. Not at all, Hammond tells him, "It began it!" The workers mounted a general strike, bringing everything to a halt. Civil war ensued. Many of the soldiers joined with the workers. As the rich saw that they were losing in the struggle they began to destroy their property, not wanting any of it to fall into the hands of their former slaves. The workers were also reckless in their destruction, despising everything that smacked of their bondage. Between them the two sides succeeded in destroying the capitalist system and all its manifestations during two years of civil war. When the fighting ended and the rich who remained alive conceded defeat, the country was in ruins. The slate was wiped clean. Men and women found themselves in a condition to start over again. As they began to re-build their lives they discovered "the production of what used to be called art." Not high art, but the art of work-pleasure. Suddenly and spontaneously they uncovered an instinct to do the best they could with the work in hand, to make it excellent, whatever it was. Old Hammond tells Morris,

> Thus at last and by slow degrees, we got pleasure into our work; then we became conscious of that pleasure, and cultivated it, and took care that we had our fill of it; and then all was gained, and we were happy. So may it be for ages and ages! [Morris, XVI, 134]

In one respect life in the twenty-first century is unchanged. Men and women in love sometimes misunderstand one another. Dick the boatman and Clara his sweetheart have grown apart but come together again. Morris himself is drawn to a woman he meets and seems to know.

She is beautiful; her name is Ellen. She has grey eyes and looks like a fairy in a fairy garden. She makes him feel young again. She is his sister Emma; for she knows, in some way that Morris is careful not to explain, that men make "stories of me to themselves – like I know you did, my friend" [Morris, XVI, 188]. The dream-vision ends when he gathers with all his new friends from the future for a grand supper, only to discover that he has disappeared.

Morris withdrew for good from the Socialist League in November 1890. It had become apparent that the anarchist members were bent on a self-destructive course and that he was not able to hold them in check any longer. Though he continued to be active in socialist affairs, he now stepped aside. For nearly ten years he had served in the vanguard of revolutionary socialism as its most visible, honorable and important member. Discouraged in his efforts to guide the movement and avoid the twin dangers of senseless destruction and mundane accommodation, he nevertheless persevered in his belief that socialism represented the best prospect for the future of humanity. With a small body of his closest friends he carried on his mission under the banner of the Hammersmith Socialist Society, literally in his own backyard at Kelmscott House.

In the last years of his life Morris continued the work of the Firm, built the Kelmscott Press, acquired a brilliant collection of illuminated manuscripts and wrote several more increasingly remote and introspective romances that fed on fond but not forgotten desire. In 1896 he died, mourned by many who appreciated his diverse talents as designer, innovator, socialist and dreamer of dreams. Admirers today still stand amazed at his inordinate energy.

Chapter 16

A childish heart there loved me once, and lo I took his love and cast his love away

In 1896 the real life of William Morris ended, and his biographical life began. Since his death, one hundred and ten years ago, there have been an enormous number of books written about him and his circle. Only six of these, however, bear importantly on the problem Morris had with his wife and their relationship with Rossetti. All six, including the one on Rossetti, are long and thorough biographies ranging from 400 to 900 pages in length. Each appears to extend or advance our understanding, yet each is limited in some essential way. None offers a clear and convincing explanation of what actually happened among Morris, his wife and their friend Rossetti.

J.W. Mackail wrote the first biography. The son-in-law of Edward and Georgie Burne-Jones, he had access to all of the important individuals in Morris's life who were still alive. His two-volume biography, published in 1899, presented a balanced, reliable and invaluable portrait. It was also very discreet. Mackail said nothing about the failure of Morris's marriage, though he might have. "How extraordinarily interesting one could make the story," he confided while writing the book, "if one were going to die the day before it was published" [J.W. Mackail to Sydney Cockerell, 7 December 1897, British Library]. Mackail left it to future biographers to hunt for the truth.

Fifty years after Mackail's book appeared Oswald Doughty published his biography of Rossetti. The book created a sensation. Doughty disclosed that Rossetti had fallen in love with Janey Morris. He recognized that Rossetti resumed writing love poetry in the late 1860s, which coincided with his increased contact with Mrs. Morris. Having no better explanation to offer, he accepted an old rumor that "Gabriel and Jane had fallen in love almost at sight and would have married if Gabriel had not felt morally bound to marry Lizzie should he ever bring himself to marry at all." In so doing, he endorsed "the cynical story" that Rossetti "ordered Morris and Jane to marry" so as to keep her in their circle. Doughty noted that the "earlier intimacy" between Janey and Rossetti revived after Morris sold Red House and moved his family to Queen Square in 1865. More precisely he suggested the beginning of 1868 as the critical turning point. "There is no indication," he said, "that Gabriel wrote any other verse in the year 1867, but in January 1868, in his sonnet for *Venus Verticordia*, there is a hint of coming change as one who turns hesitatingly, almost tearfully indeed, after profound disillusion, from the weariness of mere unhappy retrospect and stagnation to a new tremulous hope born of the first stirrings of a new or renewed but heartfelt passion" [Doughty, 238, 370, 376-7].

Oddly, Doughty did not connect these "first stirrings" with the meaning of la Pia, even though he mentioned the painting on the preceding page of his book. There, Doughty noted that Rossetti began, also in January 1868, a portrait of Janey "(significantly?) [sic] as La Pia, Dante's ill-starred lady of Siena, condemned by a cruel husband to perish amidst the pestilential exhalations of the Maremma marshes" [Doughty, 376-7]. If Doughty had explored the significance further than he did he would have seen that Rossetti's selection was not fortuitous, but pointed and deliberate. Rossetti chose to paint Janey Morris as la Pia because he saw that her husband had turned against her. In doing so, Rossetti depicted the truth: Janey was too noble not to be loved.

In 1955, after Doughty's book appeared, Edward Thompson produced the first major biography of Morris since Mackail's. Thompson was not especially concerned with the failure of Morris's marriage. He dedicated his effort instead to demonstrating that Morris was a Marxist. Nevertheless, he provided an explanation. Morris had fallen in love with a vision; he "had married not her, but a picture, an ideal from his Pre-Raphaelite dream-world." Later "when the dream passed away and he came to know her as a real person, she was not suited to the fuller relationship he then desired." In short, Janey Morris was inadequate. She lacked the capacity to love deeply or intimately. Their marriage essentially "foundered on the rock of Janey's passivity." Thompson, to his credit, refused to accept the story that Janey and Rossetti had fallen in love when they first met in 1857. "Whatever sympathy existed between the beautiful model and the romantic young painter in earlier days, Janey and Rossetti were drawn together in the late 1860s after an emotional separation had already begun to take place between her and Morris" [Thompson, 75, 158, 160].

Philip Henderson took a different tack. He believed that Morris was deeply in love with his wife and was devastated by her relationship with Rossetti. In his biography, which appeared in 1967, he cited the sonnet *Near but Far Away* written in 1867/8 as direct evidence of his love and frustration. It is the poem in which the woman sees "unspoken miseries" in the eyes of her man and draws him into paradise:

> She wavered, stopped and turned, methought her eyes,
> The deep grey windows of her heart, were wet,
> Methought they softened with new regret
>
> To note in mine unspoken miseries:
> And as a prayer from out my heart did rise
> And struggle on my lips in shame's strong net
> She stayed me, and cried "Brother!" Our lips met,
> Her hands drew me into Paradise. . . .

Henderson declared that the poem was "obviously addressed to Jane." He offered his readers no explanation of why a wife would call her husband "brother" or why, given the presumed circumstances, Morris should feel any shame. It simply didn't occur to him that the woman of the poem might be his sister. Henderson also failed to think critically about other evidence. When Philip Webb, visiting Janey Morris at Kelmscott in September 1872, witnessed some "unfortunate circumstances," Henderson suggested that Webb had seen that Janey "appeared more married to Rossetti than to Morris" [Henderson, 92, 132]. Henderson should have known that Rossetti was in Scotland, not at Kelmscott at the time.

Jack Lindsay, writing in 1975, proposed yet another view. According to Lindsay, the move from Red House in 1865 marked the beginning of the breakdown of the marriage. Morris, he wrote,

> was in fact leaving much more behind than he could have known at the time. With the loss of the dream of re-creating around himself a medieval world he lost also the love of the woman who had been for him the incarnation of the dream.

Janey could neither endure the return to a humble state nor understand her husband's ambitions. She "retreated into her refuge of illness" and soon drew Rossetti's "insidious and undemanding adoration." Responding to her rejection, Morris gravitated toward Georgie Burne-Jones for love. Their love was real but unconsummated.Lindsay wrote,

> It seems that Georgie hesitated on the brink of giving herself to Morris. This reading of the situation is supported by the poem which May [Morris] printed as *Near but Far Away*, inscribed 'May 11th, and which cannot be addressed to Janey [referring to Henderson's interpretation of the poem].

Lindsay felt that substituting Georgie for Janey adequately explained the woman's calling her lover "Brother," since Mrs. Burne-Jones refused to commit adultery. "In saying 'Brother' instead of 'Husband' or 'Beloved'," wrote Lindsay, "Georgie revives the taboo against which there is no appeal, making his exclusion final." When he wrote this passage Lindsay dismissed my argument, first made in 1972, that Morris was displaying his passion for his sister, as "untenable" [Lindsay, 138-9, 186, 188]. He provided no further comment or explanation.

In 1995 Fiona MacCarthy produced her version of the life of William Morris. MacCarthy, like Lindsay, acknowledged the point that Mackail made in his biography about Emma's early importance to Morris. "His desertion by Emma," she wrote, "and the breaking of that bonding was the beginning of, for him, a tragic cycle of female intimacy vouchsafed and then withdrawn." Morris's marriage to Janey Burden, MacCarthy believed, was for Janey a matter of convenience, not love.

> She implied she had really had no choices in the matter, given social circumstances that did not allow the acceptance or refusal of a suitor on purely emotional grounds.

Morris was a good catch, but he was limited. He could not appreciate that his wife had "an almost 1990s' instinct for being her own person, for remaking an identity" and "a craving for danger, for living on the edge." After their return to London in 1865, she began to model for Rossetti. The two "gradually edged much nearer" and eventually became lovers. In despair Morris turned to the sympathetic Georgie Burne-Jones for love. MacCarthy concluded, like Lindsay, that Mrs. Burne-Jones is the woman in the sonnet *Near but Far Away*. "There is," she wrote about the poem, "the suggestion of fleeting physicality. We can also surmise that in this sense he [the man in the poem] was rejected" [MacCarthy, 51, 141, 221-2, 250]. Her reading of the poem is extraordinary, even perverse, given that they kiss and she draws her man into Paradise.

Lindsay and MacCarthy agreed on the proper reading of another important and revealing poem, known by its opening line "Why Dost Thou Struggle." Morris wrote it from the woman's point of view. In the poem, the woman admits that she stole her childish lover's heart and treated him lightly. He was needy; it pleased her that he adored her, but she was not in love with him. Still, she found his love so sweet that in a way she loved him too. Lindsay and MacCarthy both identified the woman as Janey Morris. But this woman is not a wife. How could she be? She tells us that she never imagined that the man would play a lover's role in her life, and she certainly never intended to arouse his manly passions. The sense of the poem only comes together when we recognize that the speaker is Morris's sister.

A childish heart there loved me once, and lo
I took his love and cast his love away.

A childish greedy heart! yet still he clung
So close to me that much he pleased my pride
And soothed a sorrow that about me hung
With glimpses of his love unsatisfied –

And soothed my sorrow – but time soothed it too
Though ever did its aching fill my heart
To which the foolish child still closer drew
Thinking in all I was to have a part.

But now my heart grown silent of its grief
Saw more than kindness in his hungry eyes:

But I must wear a mask of false belief
And feign that nought I knew his miseries.

I wore a mask because though certainly
I loved him not yet was there something soft
And sweet to have him ever loving me:
Belike it is I wellnigh loved him oft –

Nigh loved him oft and needs must grant to him
Some kindness out of all he asked of me
And hoped his love would still hang vague and dim
About my life like half-heard melody.

He knew my heart and over-well knew this
And strove, poor soul, to pleasure me herein;
But yet what might he do? some doubtful kiss
Some word, some look might give him hope to win.

Poor hope, poor soul, for he again would come
Thinking to gain yet one more golden step
Toward Love's shrine, and lo the kind speech dumb
The kind look gone, no love upon my lip –

Yea gone, yet not my fault, I knew of love
But my love and not his; how could I tell
That such blind passion in him I should move?
Behold I have loved faithfully and well. . . .

[Morris, XXIV, 362-3]

"Note," Lindsay tells us after we read the poem, "how Morris looks on himself as a child" [Lindsay, 182]. Of course! The poem reaches back into the author's earliest childhood.

Like a picture puzzle containing an apparent and a hidden image the story of Morris's love life emerges clearly. As a child he fell in love with his sister. It was "natural enough that they should discover as they grew up that they were in love with one another" [Morris, I, 164]. He was crushed at age sixteen when she married. Later, at Oxford, he began to write love poems and send them to her. He envisaged her as an erotic, ideal woman who could motivate him to high purpose. But as he failed in his early efforts to make a career, his fidelity faltered. In 1857 he met Janey Burden. In her, he found someone whom he could actually love and build a family with; he hoped that she was someone who could help him transcend his adoration of Emma. Their marriage succeeded for several years. But after a serious illness in the winter of 1864 he determined that the good life of domestic bliss was not enough. He felt compelled to resume the hunt for the Holy Grail or the Golden Fleece. He began to write poetry again. In so doing he returned to his inspirational source. His love for his sister quickly re-emerged and displaced his love for his wife. Janey Morris took notice; so did their friends, including Rossetti who decided to intervene. Having lost his own wife, Rossetti tried to whip Morris into better behavior. When Morris remained unmoved, Rossetti fell in love. Janey had no desire to exchange her husband for Rossetti, but, preferring affection to neglect and indifference, she responded to his attention. Morris in turn found comfort in a lot of direct contact with Georgie Burne-Jones and Aglaia Coronio, but there is no evidence that he ever made love to either woman. His erotic attention after 1866, as it was before 1859, remained focused on his sister.

Using the mask of fiction, Morris summarized the twin nodes of his emotional life. The words are found in *News from Nowhere*. They are deliberately opaque but perfectly revealing. In his youth, before his marriage, he suffered "Calf-love, mistaken for a heroism that shall be life-long, yet early waning into disappointment." When he began writing poetry again, Emma re-appeared at the center of his life. He suddenly felt "the inexplicable desire that comes on a man of riper years to be the all-in-all to some one woman, whose ordinary human kindness and human beauty he has idealized into superhuman perfection, and made the one object of his desire" [Morris, XVI, 57].

As for Emma, we may infer that Morris described her accurately in the poem above. We believe her when she tells us "there was something soft and sweet to have him ever loving me." We can believe that she "hoped his love would still hang vague and dim about my life like half-heard melody." We have no doubt that she never intended to move "such blind passion in him" as he felt. Her closing words, echoing those of Guenevere defending her honor in Morris's early poem, ring true: "Behold I have loved faithfully and well."

After her husband and her brother died (they both passed away in 1896), Emma moved to the south coast of England. There she lived "very peacefully and happy in a little house on the cliffs at Lyme Regis, surrounded by her brother's yellow Marigold wallpapers and his blue carpets and chintzes" until her death in 1915 [Morris Collection]. In her bedroom, in the back of a bureau drawer where a niece discovered them in 1921, she kept her brother's early love poems, including the one that asks, "Do you keep your child-love, brother?"

Note on Sources

Manuscript Sources:

Morris Collection – William Morris Gallery, Walthamstow
Morris MS – British Library, William Morris Papers, MS 45,298A
Taylor Papers – National Archives, Warington Taylor Papers

Printed Sources:

Angeli – Angeli, Helen Rossetti, *Dante Gabriel Rossetti, His Friends And Enemies.* London: Hamish Hamilton, 1949.

Brown – Hueffer, Ford Madox, *Ford Madox Brown, A Record of His Life and Work.* London: Longmans Green and Co., 1896.

DGR-JM – Letters Bryson, John, ed., *Dante-Gabriel Rossetti and Jane Morris: Their Correspondence.* Oxford: Oxford University Press, 1976.

Doughty – Doughty, Oswald, *A Victorian Romantic: Dante Gabriel Rossetti.* London: Oxford University Press, 1960 [1949].

GBJ – G B-J [Georgiana Burne-Jones], *Memorials of Edward Burne-Jones.* London: Macmillan, 1904.

Glasier – Glasier, J. Bruce, *William Morris and the Early Days of the Socialist Movement.* London: Longmans Green and Co., 1921.

Henderson – Henderson, Philip, *William Morris, His Life, Work and Friends.* London: Thames and Hudson, 1967.

James Letters – Edel, Leon, ed., *Henry James Letters.* Cambridge: Harvard University Press, 1974.

Lindsay – Lindsay, Jack, *William Morris: His Life and Work*. New York: Taplinger Publishing Company, 1979 [1975].

MacCarthy – MacCarthy, Fiona, *William Morris, A Life for Our Time*. New York: Alfred A. Knoff, 1995.

Mackail – Mackail, J. W., *The Life of William Morris*. London: Longmans Green and Co., 1899.

May Morris – Morris, May, ed., *William Morris: Artist, Writer, Socialist*. Oxford: Basil Blackwell, 1936.

Morris – Morris, May, ed., *The Collected Works of William Morris*. London: Longmans Green and Co., 1910-5.

Morris Letters – Kelvin, Norman, ed., *The Collected Letters of William Morris*. Princeton: Princeton University Press, 1984-91.

Morris Letters H – Henderson, Philip, ed., *The Letters of William Morris to His Family and Friends*. London: Longmans Green, 1950.

Rossetti Letters – Doughty, Oswald and J. R. Wahl, eds., *Letters of Dante Gabriel Rossetti*. Oxford: Clarendon Press, 1965.

Rossetti Poems – Marsh, Jan, ed., *Dante Gabriel Rossetti, Collected Writings*. Chicago: New Amsterdam Books, 2000.

Swinburne Letters – Lang, Cecil Y., ed., *The Swinburne Letters*. New Haven: Yale University Press, 1959-62.

Thompson – Thompson, E.P., *William Morris, Romantic to Revolutionary*. Stanford: Standford University Press, 1988 [1955].

Webb – Lethaby, W. R., *Philip Webb and His Work*. London: Oxford University Press, 1935.

Yonge – Yonge, Charlotte, *The Heir of Redclyffe*. Oxford: Oxford University Press, 1997 [1853].

Index

About the Author

John Le Bourgeois has taught English history, been a banker and written many articles on William Morris and his circle of friends. Recently retired as Associate Dean in the Fox School of Business and Management at Temple University, he lives with his wife Mimi in Swarthmore, Pennsylvania, in the United States.